Yes!
You Really
CAN Change

Yes!
You Really
CAN Change

*What to Do When
You're Spiritually Stuck*

CHIPINGRAM

MOODY PUBLISHERS

CHICAGO

Interior Design: Puckett Smartt
Cover Design: Erik M. Peterson
Cover illustration of ligthbulbs copyright © 2019 by muchomor / iStock (1190251269). All rights reserved.

Library of Congress Cataloging-in-Publication Data

Names: Ingram, Chip, 1954- author.
Title: Yes, you really can change : what to do when you're spiritually stuck / Chip Ingram.
Description: Chicago : Moody Publishers, [2021] | Includes bibliographical references. | Summary: "If God changes lives, why is mine stuck in the mud? We all want life change, but achieving it is hard. As Christians, we know Jesus has made it possible. The Holy Spirit even lives inside us! And yet, too many Christians are going nowhere. Can things ever get better? Pastor Chip Ingram's answer is simple: Yes, you really CAN change! With practical advice drawn straight from Scripture, Chip answers questions such as: Why do so many Christians change so little? Where do we get the power to change? How do you know when you're really changing? How do you break out of a destructive lifestyle? How do you make it last? In Yes, You Really CAN Change, you'll learn the difference between living for God's approval and from God's approval. Only when you understand your full acceptance by a loving God can life change begin to happen"-- Provided by publisher.
Identifiers: LCCN 2020047553 (print) | LCCN 2020047554 (ebook) | ISBN 9780802424235 (paperback) | ISBN 9780802499868 (ebook)
Subjects: LCSH: Change (Psychology)--Religious aspects--Christianity. | Spiritual formation. | Bible. Ephesians, IV--Criticism, interpretation, etc.
Classification: LCC BV4599.5.C44 I54 2021 (print) | LCC BV4599.5.C44 (ebook) | DDC 248--dc23
LC record available at https://lccn.loc.gov/2020047553
LC ebook record available at https://lccn.loc.gov/2020047554

Originally delivered by fleets of horse-drawn wagons, the affordable paperbacks from D. L. Moody's publishing house resourced the church and served everyday people. Now, after more than 125 years of publishing and ministry, Moody Publishers' mission remains the same—even if our delivery systems have changed a bit. For more information on other books (and resources) created from a biblical perspective, go to www.moodypublishers.com or write to:

Moody Publishers
820 N. LaSalle Boulevard
Chicago, IL 60610

1 3 5 7 9 10 8 6 4 2

Printed in the United States of America

I dedicate this book to my brothers and sisters who have tried so hard to please God, to change, to break old habits, to overcome addictions, envy, private lusts, outbursts of anger yet find themselves frustrated, discouraged, and starting to believe that their life can never really change.

I have been there, and I have done that, and I have counseled untold numbers of Christians who felt the same way before they understood how lasting "life change" really happens.

May God grant you the grace to persevere, discover a community that will support you on your journey, and teach you His truth in a way that will allow you to experience the joy of being supernaturally changed from the inside out.

Contents

Is a Changed Life Really Possible?

had just finished preaching the third message of the weekend and was pretty tired. But I lit up as I saw Bobby headed my way through the crowd. He was a young man in his late twenties who had recently put his faith in Christ. He was likable, eager, sincere, and teachable, and we'd had a number of conversations over the last year or so about his new life in Christ.

He was encountering all the normal ups and downs of his new birth. He was reading the Word, had joined a men's group, and was experiencing God presence and struggling to break free of some of the patterns of his old life. He often came up after services to ask me questions or report on how things were going at work, with his girlfriend, or with life in general. But today was different.

Bobby didn't look sad or discouraged, just matter-of-fact. "Chip, I came to thank you for all your help," he said. "I really do believe in Jesus, but Christianity just isn't working for me."

"What do you mean?" I asked.

"I've tried to do all the right stuff, and it just doesn't work for me. I keep thinking the same old thoughts, struggling with the same old sins, and feel worse now than before I became a Christian." My attempts to probe and reason with him fell on deaf ears. He had made up his mind. I drove home from church slowly and feeling sad.

I've met very few people who were as honest and straightforward as Bobby, but I've met hundreds who feel the same way. They are sincere and love God, but Christianity "is not working for them" either.

People say it a thousand different ways, but it can be summarized in just a few words. For some, it's spiritual fatigue. Their faith has stalled. They're stuck, not growing, and out of energy. For others, it's spiritual frustration. They are frustrated with their inability to overcome some private sin or maintain some spiritual discipline. They feel like a failure with no hope in sight. Still others are spiritually and emotionally exhausted from trying to measure up by praying more, reading the Bible more, giving more, serving more, and being at church more.

All these people have tried or are still trying to be really good Christians. They are sincere and are genuinely born again. But they are tired, frustrated, and wondering where the joy of their salvation is, where that promised "abundant life" is hiding. The pattern that follows is very predictable:

Try hard, do good, . . . fail.

Try harder, do good, . . . fail.

Try even harder, do good, . . . fail.

And finally, try hard, do good, . . . fake it.

These sincere followers of Jesus do not necessarily doubt their salvation or want to abandon their faith, but it's clearly not working. After some initial transformation and the cleaning up of some external, visible sins, they find themselves in bondage to private thoughts that human willpower can't change.

Over time, accommodation becomes a lifestyle. Envy, jealousy, greed, lust, coveting, and comparing ourselves with others are so widespread within the church—and so few Christians seem to have overcome them—that we reframe our struggles in psychological language. Our lack of success is so common that it seems "normal."

Deep issues of the heart, strongholds, and damage from our past tend to get buried as we smile, go to church somewhat regularly, read the Bible occasionally, and try very hard to be nice people. God gradually seems more distant, nagging guilt becomes more persistent, and times of extended, intimate prayer are few and far between.

It all happens so subtly, and what was once a passionate relationship with Jesus is now not much more than sin and image management, in which a believer becomes more focused on appearing loving and humble than actually loving people or being humble.

It all happens so subtly, and what was once a passionate relationship with Jesus is now not much more than sin and image management, in which a believer becomes more focused on appearing loving and humble than actually loving people or being humble.

That kind of Christian life is joyless and weighed down with duty, and all the church activities and disciplines feel more like a second job than a dynamic relationship with the living God.

Sound familiar? If so, and if you're beginning to feel guilty or wondering how I could know all these things about you, please don't be discouraged, and please read on. I have lived the life I'm describing. I hated it, and I hated me in the process.

It wasn't intentional by those who discipled me, but somewhere along the line, I came to believe that God's love and acceptance were conditional on Bible reading, long prayers, church activities, memorizing Scripture, giving my money away, and sharing my faith. My overachieving personality and workaholic tendencies played into these misbeliefs in ways that created an image of godliness and devotion but were privately crushing my soul.

The joy I had as a new Christian was gone. The duties, the obligations, the responsibilities, and my unsuccessful efforts to overcome my internal, private sins made the Christian life unbearable. In desperation, I officially "quit"—and told God so about two years into my walk with Him.

Little did I know that coming to that point of realizing I simply "can't live the Christian life" was the beginning of the abundant, joy-filled life that Christ had promised. I had been living *for* God's approval rather than *from* God's approval. And that makes all the difference in the world.

After more than thirty-five years of pastoring God's people, my heart aches for those who are stalled, stuck, exhausted, fatigued, and frustrated. These fellow believers really love the Lord Jesus, but in moments of honest reflection would admit, "The Christian life is not working for me."

This book is good news!

It is time-tested in my life and through my teaching to millions of people around the world who were stalled, stuck, exhausted, frustrated, and fatigued in their walk with God.

> **I had been living for *God's approval* rather than from *God's approval*. And that makes all the difference in the world.**

The teaching is rooted in one of the most profound chapters in the New Testament. It explains God's supernatural transformation process. We will learn that radical life-change is for everyone, how it actually happens in everyday life, what part God does that we can't do, and what part we do that He won't do.

You'll learn why we all get stuck at

times and how to get unstuck when we find ourselves falling into old patterns or believing old lies.

This book is about hope!

It's about becoming who Jesus saved you to become. It's about change that's real, powerful, supernatural, and available to every child of God.

There are no magic bullets or quick formulas, no promises of ease or success and prosperity if you simply follow steps 1, 2, and 3. But if you really want to know God, experience His love, and be changed from the inside out by His power rather than your "trying harder and harder," this book is for you.

If you long to experience the fruit of God's Spirit working in you and your relationships as you find yourself becoming more loving, experiencing more peace, filled with joy (even in difficult circumstances), finding kind words coming out of your mouth toward people who irritate you as Christ lives His life through you . . . then you're in for the journey of a lifetime.

I can't wait to begin this life-changing adventure with you, so let me introduce you to our teacher and our guide.

A Dramatic Experience of Change

Saul left Jerusalem on a mission, and no one could have expected the enormous change that was coming to his life. Of all people, his reputation and his determination made him the least likely candidate for transformation. If anyone could stamp out a growing movement with resolve, it was him.

A divine encounter can change a lot. Saul only made it partway to Damascus because a blinding vision of Jesus stopped him in his tracks. Jesus asked this young rabbi why he was persecuting Him, and Saul, a.k.a. Paul, didn't have an answer. Instead, he soon learned that he would be carrying the name of Jesus to Gentiles and

Jews as a chosen instrument of God. His life had just taken a radical turn in the opposite direction of his convictions.

We read about Paul's ministry throughout much of Acts and in the words of his own letters to churches around the Mediterranean world. We don't know much about his life before his conversion, but he pours out plenty of details of his post-conversion life in his writings. Page after page tells us of the drastic, comprehensive changes in his life.

A divine encounter can change a lot.

One of the reasons Paul is so fascinating to us is that he experienced the kind of transformation most of us long for. We see a clear distinction between old and new in his life. He was an enemy of Christians, yet became perhaps the most zealous Christian of them all. He was steeped in the intricacies of Jewish law, then an ardent advocate for the gospel of grace that brings the law to completion. He was a persecutor who became the persecuted. His old anger turned to lasting joy. The contrast is so clear and convincing that he stands as an enduring testimony of what Jesus can do to change lives.

When we first come to Christ, we want to experience change too. It's a desire God has placed within us, and for a time, we anticipate the kind of transformation we read about in the New Testament. Many of us experience tastes and glimpses of it. But somewhere along the way, most of us become frustrated with the process. Some people struggle so much that they start wondering if change is even possible. The power of the gospel that invaded our lives at conversion seems strangely absent in the thick of daily life.

God has not left us there without help. In fact, Paul himself tells us how to experience the kind of change we long for. And he should know. His personal transformation was a startling testimony to the early church.

While we know about Paul's radical conversion, we know relatively little about the period that followed. Several years passed between his conversion and his public ministry, and we can only imagine the changes he experienced during that time—how the new life worked its way into his heart and mind, how his ways of thinking and living changed from that first encounter with Jesus to his maturity as Jesus' follower. He doesn't give us much biographical information about those years—he leaves a few hints in a couple of his letters—but he does dissect the spiritual process for us. He shows us what transformation looks like and spells out many of the details.

We will explore that journey of transformation in this book, looking at it through Paul's eyes and learning from his letters how our own lives can genuinely change. It's a process many Christians are either unfamiliar with or have lost the hope of experiencing. But it is real, and it is part of our salvation as believers in Jesus.

In order to understand how our lives change as Christians, we first need to explore some of the reasons so many Christians' lives don't. Why are people like Bobby giving up? Why do so many believers beat themselves up emotionally for falling short of godly ideals? Why do many Christians, including church leaders, become addicted to pornography? If the fundamental message of the New Testament is change—that everyone in Christ is a new creation and all things have become new (2 Cor. 5:17)—why aren't all of us experiencing that kind of transformation?

People are genuinely becoming Christian and seeing change for a while, but even a quick look at the spiritual landscape tells us that many Christians are not living much differently from nonbelievers.

People are genuinely becoming Christian and seeing change for a while, but even a quick look at the spiritual landscape tells us that many Christians are not living much differently from nonbelievers. Some have become so used to a lack of change that they begin to wonder if it's possible.

Is Radical Life-Change Possible Today?

Genuine, lasting life-change is not an ancient myth. It is absolutely possible today. Many Christians throughout history, including right now, have experienced it. That's actually the distinguishing mark of the Christian faith—radically transformed lives over time. The testimonies of people saved from the depths of sin are true, and they aren't only for those from extreme backgrounds. Any believer at any time can begin to experience the kind of change the New Testament promises.

I think the reason so many people don't is that we've believed a lot of things that have taken us in the wrong direction. I certainly experienced that cycle of "try hard, do good, fail" in my early years as a Christian. I quickly learned that a lot of people were experiencing the same thing but had simply gotten to the "fake it" stage before I did. Yet deep down inside, every human being longs for real change. It's in our spiritual DNA. We crave it in our fallen condition, and when we come to Christ, the Holy Spirit breathes those longings into us anew. God has made us to want change. That's why the self-help industry is a multibillion-dollar industry. We want to live better, think better, look better, relate better, and experience more. We were made in the image of God, and we're instinctively trying to get back to it.

I imagine you've experienced these longings yourself. You've probably also experienced the struggles that come with them. The good news is that change really is possible, and God wants you to experience it. He is on your side in this transformation process. And if God is on your side, who can be against you (Rom. 8:31)? The obstacles are not too great. God's promises are not uncertain. And His power is not lacking. The only thing most people are missing is an understanding of God's transformational process—knowing how to experience the kind of change promised in our new birth and new life in Christ.

The gospel of Jesus Christ really does change lives when we know how to apply it and let the power of God work in us. The lack of transformation in many Christians' lives is not the fault of Jesus or His Word. There is nothing defective in the gospel, no missing information, no secret to change that hasn't already been revealed. There are certain principles and practices to change that we will explore throughout this book, but they aren't lacking in the biblical message. Far too many people have experienced the kind of radical transformation depicted and promised in the Bible for us to wonder whether it's true.

You can be confident that this radical transformation is not just for a select few people who happen to be especially touched by God's power. It's for you. This is your inheritance as a believer in Jesus. God is calling you—and will enable you—to live as a new creation.

Change really is possible, but it's important to understand the kind of change God promises. He does not want simply to clean up your outside, improve your morals, give you some stronger relationships, and teach you Christian lingo. He will affect every area of your life, but this is not about being absorbed into a Christian subculture or wearing a different face. The kind of transformation He wants for you begins on the inside and works its way out. It reshapes your heart and desires, fills you with His wisdom, power, and love, and forms the character of Jesus within you. It does affect your exterior, but it goes much deeper. Jesus did not come to tell you how to be the best version of yourself. He came to make you new. That's what you've longed for, and that's what God promises.

That's the kind of change we will be exploring in the following chapters. It's a supernatural transformation that can only occur as we participate with the Holy Spirit working within us. When we begin to experience that change daily and consistently, we find ourselves on a journey that moves us from old to new, from ordinary to extraordinary, from "I'm only human" to "I'm becoming like Jesus." This is not only possible; it's part of our salvation, available for everyone who believes. It is what we were designed for.

Our guide through this process is the apostle who experienced such a radical change himself. In the fourth chapter of his letter to the Ephesians, he gives us a template for transformation that is rooted in the love and purposes of God and delivered to us through the mercies and work of Christ.

We will look at that template in its amazing context and in its profound depth, drawing from many other biblical insights to understand the power God puts within us, the calling we have to live in it, and the specific tools we can put into place to experience all He has for us. When we grasp what Jesus did at the cross, understand the role of other believers in our growth, and begin practicing the principles God gives us, we will see the miracle of life-change occurring deep inside and working its way out into the rest of our lives.

Whether you are a new Christian full of hope for radical life-change, a seasoned believer disappointed or frustrated with your journey so far, or a Christian who has experienced some lasting change but simply longs for more, I am convinced that Paul's words will give you helpful tools to implement the power of the gospel in your day-to-day life. If you follow the biblical principles of change laid out in his letters and elsewhere in the New Testament, you can experience it just as Paul and multitudes of other Christians throughout history have. The transformation you long for is not only possible. It's promised.

My prayer as you read this book is that you will see God's promises in a new way—that your desire for lasting life-change and the fullness of salvation will become more and more real in your experience. I trust that you will discover the wisdom and insight you have searched for and that your desire to live as a new creation will be fulfilled. And I believe that if you put that wisdom into practice, your life and the lives of many who know you—will never be the same.

CHAPTER 1

Why Do So Many Christians Change So Little?

The world is full of promises of change. Advertisers hawk products and services that are said to be able to renew your youth, change your appearance, create a new lifestyle, fix your body, improve your mood, make your life easier, and enhance your relationships. They all promise some form of change that will make your life better. But the people who buy into those promises very often end up disappointed—and looking for a new change.

Politicians run their campaigns on promises of change. Since few people are completely happy with the status quo, the most effective political platforms promise to end it. So new waves of leaders are swept into office from time to time, and before long, most voters find themselves still disappointed with the status quo. The next time elections roll around, they vote for more change.

We even promise change to ourselves. Every year as New Year's Day approaches, millions of people vow to make the changes they've been longing and needing to make. They resolve to eat better, exercise more, read certain books, quit certain habits, or take better vacations. Christians may resolve to read the Bible or pray more consistently, both of which greatly increase the possibility of lasting change. Yet sometime around February, if not sooner, many of those resolutions are long broken and maybe even forgotten, and no matter how many "starting points" we set for ourselves during the year, we often find ourselves facing the next New Year with the same set of resolutions.

The gospel promises change too. The Bible assures us that those who are in Christ are new creations—that old things have passed away, and all things have now become new (2 Cor. 5:17). Many people throughout history and today have experienced radical transformation; their testimonies and examples inspire us to keep believing and hoping for radical transformation in our lives too. Yet the church is also filled with numerous people who haven't changed much at all. And if we're honest, most of us can testify that as much as our faith in Jesus as our Savior has changed us, there are still huge areas of our lives that remain frustratingly unchanged.

Polling research by the Barna Group and Gallup tells us that multitudes of people in the Western world who claim to know Jesus as their Savior have not experienced much change in terms of the way they live their lives, the decisions they make, and the character they demonstrate. Some polls have indicated very little difference between Christian and non-Christian divorce rates, family lives, de-structive behaviors, and spiritual vitality. More recent polls that account for levels of Christian commitment suggest some significant differences; people who regularly go to church, read their Bibles, pray, and discuss spiritual issues at home actually do have significantly lower divorce rates, fewer addictive behaviors, and more satisfying relationships. But that's about 10 to 20 percent of the American church, which leaves quite a few Christians who are struggling with failing families, personal chaos, and addictions like pornography, workaholism, infidelity, and spiritual stagnancy. In many sectors of the church, and in many individual lives, something is very wrong.

What are we to make of that? Is the gospel just one of those promises that ultimately disappoints? Is it the religious equivalent of ambitious advertising, hopeful campaign rhetoric, and personal New Year's resolutions? Have millions, even billions of Christians bought into a false hope of genuine, lasting change?

The problem is not a lack of desire. In my experience, most true Christians have experienced at least some degree of change at some point in their lives and have longed for more. But somewhere along the way, they lost momentum, enthusiasm, and a sense of progress. They grew fatigued and frustrated. Many have had visions of continuous growth, only to experience lots of ups and downs and fall far short of their ideals. Many have never even gotten off the ground to begin with, slipping into old ways of life soon after believing. Yet the promises of God in Scripture remain. The gospel is all about change, and our longings are real. We really do become new creations. So how does that reality play out in our lives?

That's where many Christians are struggling. I can certainly relate to that, and I suspect you can too. How can we claim that Jesus makes a difference in our lives when our lives don't look much different from the society around us? Or, more personally, how can we claim that Jesus makes a difference in our lives when we keep struggling with the same problems and feel frustratingly, achingly unchanged? Many people long for the kind of change that comes with being a new creation. Few are experiencing it. Why?

The Problem of Passive Faith

Before we begin exploring the nuts and bolts of genuine life-change, let's dig a little deeper into the root of the problems that prevent it. Why do so many Christians experience so little change?

Perhaps it comes from living in a traditionally semi-Christian culture in which people go to church, sit still for an hour or two, sing a few songs, listen to a sermon, nod their heads in agreement, assume that their agreement equals faith, and go home living just as they did before—and just as their nonchurchgoing friends do. That's a passive kind of faith, and it keeps people in touch with cultural Christianity. But it doesn't change lives.

When the pursuit of bigger, better, and more dominates our thoughts and activities, it inhibits and undermines the changes God wants to work into our lives.

An hour or two of worship and teaching on Sundays is good, but it is rarely enough to combat the steady stream of un-Christian perspectives that fill our workplaces, communities, media, and interactions with society and culture at large. And that steady stream can be seductive. Many Christians have bought into the lie that we can be satisfied and fulfilled with a little more money, a better job, a successful family with kids who excel, a coveted neighborhood, nicer clothes, a remodeled house, a better car, and better vacations. All those things can be wonderful blessings given by God, but they can also become idols that compel our hearts to keep reaching for more and never having enough. When the pursuit of bigger, better, and more dominates our thoughts and activities, it inhibits and undermines the changes God wants to work into our lives. We eventually find that bigger, better, and more never really satisfies, and the change that would have satisfied us remains elusive.

Millions of Christians have settled for the emptiness of worldly pursuits by prioritizing them over the adventure of walking with God and experiencing the transformation He gives. Jesus promised that when we seek God's kingdom and righteousness above all else, all else tends to fall into place (Matt. 6:33). Unfortunately, passive faith tends to reverse that order. Those who seek the kingdom of God first get that and more; those who seek worldly pursuits above the kingdom of God usually miss out on the satisfaction of both. As C. S. Lewis wrote, "You can't get second things by putting them first; you can get second things only by putting first things first."[1] Many Christians have found that to be painfully true.

If any of the above describes your experience, don't despair. Passive faith is an easy pattern to fall into, and Jesus warned that it's powerfully seductive, but it doesn't mean you've failed. It just means you've gradually been affected by cultural and social trends that thwart God's transforming work in your life. There's no condemnation for those who are in Christ. If you recognize this pattern in your life, the good news is that recognizing it is the first step to changing it. Your heavenly Father is ready and waiting for you to turn to Him and enter into a deeper and more fulfilling relationship with Him.

In my many years of pastoring and leading ministries, I have become convinced that many people are not intentionally distancing themselves from God. They just don't understand or know how to apply biblical truth to their lives. Far too many people fit Paul's description of "having a form of godliness but denying its power" (2 Tim. 3:5). The average professing believer can affirm that Jesus died on the cross, rose from the grave, and saved us from our sins. Most can point to a time when they accepted Christ by faith as their Savior and asked Him into their hearts. But many who have experienced an initial change of perspective and lifestyle ceased to grow significantly in ways that impact their core values and character. Jesus has not made a significant difference in the way many Christians live—how they spend their time, handle their sexuality, live with integrity, determine their priorities, fulfill their roles in marriage and parenting, love their neighbors as themselves, and seek to reach the world for Christ. The church as a whole desperately needs to experience the fullness of God and His power to transform us.

Receiving the free gift of salvation is a huge, foundational decision, but it is a starting point for the rest of our lives, not the culmination of our faith. The cross and resurrection save us from the penalty of sin when we believe, but they are also meant to save us from sin's influence in our lives from that day forward. It's great to know what we were saved *from*, but we also need to discover what we were saved *for*. God has redeemed us so He can restore us into His image. We were saved in order to experience a holy transformation that not only changes our own lives but also the lives of people around us.

Unfortunately, evangelical Christianity has developed a culture in which no one is very surprised when someone prays to receive Christ and continues in a lifestyle of minimal change. For many, this may reflect a casual approach to faith, but I think most genuine believers feel stuck in a dilemma. On one hand, they know that Christ is living within them. On the other, they continue to struggle with sin and get swept into the influences of their culture.

My heart goes out to people caught in that dilemma because I know from experience what it feels like. They go back and forth between wondering whether something is wrong with them or with the gospel itself. Many haven't connected with other believers who could help them, developed new habits that allow transformation to occur, or learned the principles of spiritual growth. Over time, that ongoing dilemma leads to a life of resignation—Christian in name, but agnostic toward how it all works. They hope they go to heaven but wish they could experience its power on earth. Little by little, the new life fades back into the old, and even though they hunger for change from time to time, they have little hope of experiencing it. They resign themselves to passive faith.

Why Is Change So Elusive?

Why are so many Christians missing out on authentic, supernatural, spiritual transformation? Why is there such a gap between the picture we are given in Scripture and the picture of so many Christians' lives? Why does transformation seem so difficult and beyond reach?

Jesus met a man who had been paralyzed for thirty-eight years (John 5:1–15). The man had been lying near the pool of Bethesda, where the waters were thought to have healing power whenever they were stirred by an angel. Many blind, paralyzed, and sick people positioned themselves at the pool's edge so they could be the first one in when the water moved. But this man had a problem. He said he couldn't get to the water first because he had no one to help him. He had managed to put himself in proximity of a major transformation but not close enough to actually experience it. So he remained paralyzed, unable to do anything about his condition, with change just out of reach.

Does that sound familiar? That's not a bad description of the dilemma many people face, longing for the idea of change but perhaps reluctant or even paralyzed to take the steps that would actually create it. Jesus, who had looked into the hearts of so many other people and pointed out their true thoughts and motivations, clearly understood this man's predicament. He knew the problem, and He knew how to fix it. But He asked the lame man a penetrating question: "Do you want to get well?" (John 5:6). And the man never really gave Him a straight answer. He responded only with an excuse for why change wasn't possible.

Jesus' question seems obvious on the surface. Anybody seeing a paralyzed man at the edge of a pool known for healing would assume he wanted to get well. But the human desire for change is rarely that simple. Change means leaving some familiar things behind, and many people are afraid to do that. That's one reason so many people feel stuck in dysfunctional relationships and avoid dealing with the dysfunction, or why employees discontent in their work don't go to the trouble to seek a new position and instead remain where they are. It's what they know. The benefit of change is that it allows for a new way of life. The problem with change is that it demands a new way of life. It isn't an easy fix.

We also have to battle our own physiology. Our brains are wired for habits. That is very helpful most of the time; it means we don't have to relearn everything we know and do every single day. But it also means that developing new ways of thinking and doing things can be very difficult. Neurologists tell us that established neural pathways work to overcome new, developing pathways, and the only way the new ones can become established is through strong conviction and persistence in renewing our minds. That's why time and consistency are so important in our change processes. Far too many people give up before the new becomes a part of their lives.

Motivation and neurology aside, I think there are at least three primary reasons Christians fail to change as thoroughly as Scripture promises: spiritual ignorance, spiritual isolation, and spiritual myopia.

Spiritual Ignorance

Many Christians simply don't know who they are. They don't understand their identity in Christ, the new nature they have been given, the foundation of grace God has provided, and the Spirit who lives within them. As a result, they revert to old-nature strategies: try hard, do good, fail, and try again. Those strategies come early in life; most of us have been trained from an early age in a punishment-and-reward system. We experience negative consequences for bad behavior, but we are given incentives and rewards for good behavior. So it's only natural that we would apply the same psychology of behavior to our relationship with God.

But that's not the kind of relationship God has given us. Jesus already took the punishment for our sins, united us with Him in resurrected life, and made us His coheirs so we can receive the rewards He deserves. That's part of what it means to be "in Christ." He exchanged His life for ours, taking our sin upon Himself and giving us His own righteousness. He paid the price for us, and we enter into the life He has given. When we act as if our relationship with God is based on our behavior, we are stepping out of that grace and reverting to old ways. We have to know who we are in Him and live from the new righteousness He has provided.

The biblical word for being made right with God is *justification*. That's what happens the moment we receive Christ. We are justified. God takes all the sin and guilt in the debt column of our lives and marks it "paid in full." This isn't just a wave of a wand or an arbitrarily canceled debt. It is based on what Jesus did on the cross. He took the penalty of our sins upon Himself, and when we receive Him by faith, that sacrifice applies to our relationship with God. Everything is paid for. Not only that, the righteousness of Jesus was deposited into our account, so God sees us as holy and pure in Him. That's our legal standing before God (Acts 13:39; Rom. 3:24, 28). We can't add to that standing or take away from it. It's ours—a gift of grace.

The biblical word for living out that justification—demonstrating the righteousness that has already been given to us—is *sanctification*. It simply means being "set apart" to God. In one sense, we have already been sanctified—set apart and made holy. But in a practical sense, it's an ongoing and lifelong process by which God changes our heart and life from the inside out to conform our character to the image of His Son (Rom. 8:29; 1 Thess. 5:23). Like being given a new wardrobe that doesn't fit us now, we are given sanctification and then spend our lives growing into it.

But that's where the problems arise. Many Christians don't

know how to grow into it. How do we make use of the grace God has given? Why do we keep sinning if God already forgave us and cleanses us? How do we live as new creations in our old, sin-saturated environment? If we don't know the answers to those questions, we will revert to the try hard, do good for a while, fail, then try again cycle. Eventually that turns into trying hard and faking it—or just giving up.

The pattern of "trying hard, doing good" for a time, and then failing can be terribly disheartening.

For the first two years of my Christian life, I lived in two worlds. On Thursday nights, I would sing praises to God in the living room of a bricklayer who led our campus ministry. On Friday nights, I would barhop with my basketball teammates all over town. I was miserable, plagued by a never-ending cycle of failure, guilt, depression, repentance, resolutions to never do that again, another try, and back to failure again. I had tasted the reality and freedom of my new life in Christ. Living out that reality was another matter. God brought some great people and some biblical teaching into my life that broke this vicious cycle. Unfortunately, many Christians are still stuck in it.

The pattern of "trying hard, doing good" for a time, and then failing can be terribly disheartening. I've heard the same laments again and again from numerous Christians:

"I try to read my Bible every day, but I miss sometimes and get off track."

"I try to conquer my lusts, but they keep coming back."

"I try to pray, but I'm not getting answers, and I lose heart."

"I try to be patient, but I keep losing my temper."

The variations are limitless, but the dynamics are always the same. This is willpower Christianity, and no matter how long it succeeds, one failure makes the whole effort feel as if it is "unsuccessful."

A 90-percent success rate isn't enough if frequent or even occasional failures seem to put us back at square one.

About a year and a half into my Christian life, I was so frustrated with my failures that I actually tried to quit. I got stuck in that dilemma between "something's wrong with me" and "the gospel isn't working." I didn't realize it was a lack of knowledge about God, His Word, and the sanctification process. I needed to learn how to tap into God's grace and power. I believe millions of believers across our country are living in that kind of defeat because they don't know what God teaches us about how holy transformation works in everyday life.

The process of sanctification requires us to walk by faith, and walking by faith necessarily involves responding to the alerts and prompts of Scripture. When God's Word shines light on a problem in us, it opens up a conversation with Him. We ask Him what it looks like to trust Him in a particular situation, relationship, or problem and read and listen for His answers. But it is important not to focus only on the issue itself. Focusing on our sin and struggles intensifies them. We need to turn our focus instead to whichever of God's promises apply to the temptation or struggle we're going through. Then we walk with Him by faith through that situation. As we apply these promises as our source of strength to address these issues, we are walking by faith. That's the core of Christian living, and we are changed in the process.

You can't live this life of faith by just reading the Bible a little bit here and there. As I've counseled hundreds of believers over the years—many with significant financial, relational, and moral problems—I generally ask them about their intake of God's Word. The answer is almost always the same: little or no personal devotion or study. Life-change demands that you make every effort to work the truth of God's Word into your heart. That should be one of your life goals as a believer: to master the contents and truths of the Bible. I know it's a big book. But if you're like many people, you are well versed in the nightly news, sports stats, the latest in movies and music, or whatever your special interests happen to be. You probably already know how to be a zealous student of your culture and your times. So why not take some of that energy and attention and apply it to something that matters for eternity?

If Bible reading feels like an item on a to-do list that reminds us how far we're falling short, it becomes a chore that interrupts our downtime. No wonder it's so easy to neglect it. But as we learn to make it a conversation with the God of the universe that deepens and directs us, it can become the highlight of our day. And if we supplement that conversation with some study helps, commentaries, and devotionals, it becomes all the richer. Over time, we begin to notice some significant changes in our perspectives, attitudes, and choices.

Immersing yourself in Scripture and choosing to believe what God says about you will radically reorient your thinking. Sadly, too many Christians are trying to overcome their sin by targeting and focusing on their sin. But that's still a preoccupation with sin, isn't it? When you keep kicking yourself for your sins, you reinforce them by giving them so much attention. If you see yourself as a helpless sinner, you'll continue to live that vision out. But God says to consider yourself dead to sin and alive to God (Rom. 6). He says you are a new creation (2 Cor. 5:17). He replaces your shame with honor, your ashes with beauty, and your mourning with praise (Isa. 61:3). He says He removes your sins as far as the east is from the west (Ps. 103:12) and has canceled out your debts (Col. 2:14). He has given you the divine nature (2 Peter 1:4). It can feel really irresponsible not to fixate on your sin—as if you're failing to police yourself—but doing so lines up with what God says and gives Him and you an opportunity to fill your mind with something else. It's the only way to break the cycle.

That's what immersing ourselves in biblical truth can do for us. It doesn't happen overnight, and there are still some practical steps to take. But spiritual ignorance is not bliss. God wants better for you.

Spiritual Isolation

A second reason many Christians don't change is spiritual isolation—a failure to be deeply engaged In Christ centered, honest relationships. By God's design, transformation normally happens in the context of community. There are very few exceptions. We experience change when we participate in regular, loving, accountable relationships centered on God's Word.

This requires faith, courage, and discernment. Not all Christian communities are mature enough to handle transparency and the flaws of their members without making judgments and creating false hierarchies of spirituality. Authenticity can be risky because grace is sometimes lacking in Christian relationships. But when you find brothers and sisters in Christ who are filled with grace, patience, and humility, and who understand the importance of mutual accountability, I encourage you to take a step of faith to open up and grow together. God uses the gifts, knowledge, and experience of other believers to help us learn to trust Him. We overcome the issues in our lives because God gives grace through His Word, His Spirit, and His people. When we realize we are totally accepted—by God and other believers—we live out our faith by grace, the same way we were saved.

Creating the right environment for safe, authentic relationships is central to helping others mature spiritually. Parents can set up their children for life transformation by regular conversations and warm interactions that flow from reading Scripture together and modeling the importance of God's Word. These times can be brief, relational, and even lighthearted at times; you don't have to fill them with information or be able to answer all their questions. Bible storybooks, family devotionals, and private conversations can become treasured memories and have lifelong impact. Family is the most important small group God ever designed.

Most spiritual isolation is caused by a subtle form of pride—not the flagrant pride of an arrogant person but the kind of pride that elevates personal agendas and priorities above God's stated purposes for our lives. When *my* work, *my* time, *my* goals squeeze God's Word and authentic spiritual relationships out of my schedule, I end up with shallow relationships, isolated from the transforming grace we receive when we serve and give of ourselves sacrificially. I know I've lived that life and, as a pastor for more than three decades, counseled countless others who have done the same. The pursuit of happiness through possessions, lifestyle, status, or independence leaves us pretty unhappy. We miss out on God's means for transformation.

The world is filled with driven, talented people who have done that—who have reached the pinnacle of success and find themselves lonely, isolated, and depressed. They have missed out on meaningful relationships on their way to getting everything they thought they wanted, only to find out they really wanted meaningful relationships. Even if they accepted Christ and go to church, they usually haven't changed much. They haven't been able to enjoy the miracle of being a new creation.

It isn't just a good idea to have a few close friends with whom you can really share your heart. Biblical, Christ-centered relationships are essential components of the Christian life. This is where most of our transformation occurs. The people who are too busy for those kinds of relationships end up being the "average" American

Christian whose life doesn't look much different from a nonbeliever's. They may be saved, but they aren't really experiencing their salvation. And they aren't becoming more and more like Jesus because they aren't walking with people who can model Christlikeness for them, hold them accountable, and help them grow.

The people who have had the greatest impact on me are those who have loved me enough to speak truth to me, even when it hurt. I'll never forget an early morning meeting at McDonald's with my mentor. He opened his Bible and read Proverbs 27:5–6—"Better is open rebuke than hidden love. Wounds from a friend can be trusted, but an enemy multiplies kisses." Then, with tears in his eyes, he pointed out a pattern of pride and arrogance that I was totally unaware of. It hurt deeply. I didn't like it. I mentally fought against it as it came out of his mouth, but the Holy Spirit spoke through him, and it was a major turning point in my life.

It isn't easy to hear a friend tell you that you're being arrogant or insensitive or too hard on your wife or kids. But that's love. That kind of accountability has spared me untold heartache. And it only happens in deep, honest, vulnerable relationships that take time and effort to develop.

Being in some kind of growth group—a small group that studies the Bible and prays together, a ministry team, or an accountability group—is perhaps the most important thing you can do for your spiritual transformation. And it's the example Jesus gave us. He came to transform the world, and He didn't set up a classroom, write a book, develop a seminar, create an online course, or advertise a program. He started a small group of men and lived with them for three years. Others followed, many learned, but the core group that spent all their time with Him were transformed the most during those years. He lived with them, modeled life for them, shared God's Word with them, and walked with them through their doubts, questions, spiritual successes, and worst failures.

That's how I learned what the Christian life looks like. After college, I lived with the family of the man who discipled me. I learned about marriage by watching him interact with his wife. I saw how he parented his children. I noticed how he served people. I watched him stop and help someone change a tire on a rainy day when the leaders of a Christian conference we had just attended all drove on by. He didn't just teach me truth; he exemplified it. It's often said that truth and faith are "more caught than taught," and it's true. We change in the context of relationships with people who teach, model, and live truth together. As one mentor told me, "Show me your friends, and I'll show you your future."

Spiritual Myopia

Myopia is nearsightedness, the inability to see clearly at a distance. One of the reasons many Christians do not experience the life-change they envision is their overdeveloped focus on immediate, up-close motivations. Sometimes they want to be more Christlike because it would lead to greater joy and fulfillment, because they want God to use them for His purposes, or because they want to avoid feeling guilty for not growing. Those desires can motivate us for a time, but they rarely last. Why? Because they aren't big enough.

Spiritual myopia subtly and insidiously makes spiritual progress a personal matter that's no one else's business. It misses the big picture—a vision of the majesty of God, the testimony of the body of Christ in the world, His desire to manifest His wisdom, power, and love in every believer. The world watches and wonders. *Is Christianity legitimate? Is the Holy Spirit real? Is the church different from any other religious organization? Is there a God who loves me and watches over me? Can I hope for heaven?* We can develop all the theological arguments we want, learn the art and logic of apologetics, and make our case for Christianity, but none of that creates a testimony as powerful as our lifestyle. The greatest evidence for Christianity is Christians. And if we are living ingrown, self-centered, typical lives that blend in with the rest of our culture, we are misrepresenting the nature of God, the salvation of Jesus, and the calling of the church. Or, as Jesus would put it (Matt. 5:13–16), the salt has lost its saltiness and the light is hidden from the world.

In many sectors of society and the church, Christianity has been reduced to a system of how-to lists or a moral and ethical code that isn't much different from society's best standards. It has become a collection of advice and hacks

> *Spiritual myopia subtly and insidiously makes spiritual progress a personal matter that's no one else's business.*

for how to have a happy life, a wonderful marriage, good kids, financial security, and the approval of a somewhat distant God. There's nothing wrong with having good relationships and a comfortable lifestyle, but those are best seen as byproducts of the faith, not its substance. They are not the essence or purpose of God's call.

There's another aspect to our myopia that can also inhibit change. Much of Christian teaching in certain periods of history, including ours, has narrowed the gospel down to spiritual salvation and nothing else, as if God is only concerned about our souls but not the practical details of our lives. Many believers have therefore subconsciously divided their lives into the spiritual and everything else. But most people find, after being saved, that they really need help with the everything else, not just the spiritual. They have problems with relationships, health, finances, decision-making, and every other area of their lives. We forget that Jesus never talked about the gospel of salvation in isolation. He talked about the kingdom of God. That covers a lot. It is relevant to every aspect of our lives here and now as well as in eternity. It's comprehensive.

We are made for eternity but placed in this space-and-time world. We are called both to know and love God forever and to demonstrate His character, nature, and salvation in our here-and-now lives. Biblical Christianity gives us answers to life's deepest questions about why we are here, the meaning of life, and our ultimate destiny, and God calls us to live as the answers to those questions in the midst of our society. When we get a high view of God, grapple with and grow in understanding of His sovereign purposes in creation and redemption, and recapture the wonder and awe of His majesty, we grow. Change happens. We realize where we fit in His larger purposes and live them out in front of a watching world. And our myopia is healed.

The Testimony of a Transformed Life

The non-Christian world raises many intellectual and philosophical objections to Christianity, but much of the dialogue about our faith in our society centers on character issues. Many people perceive Christians as judgmental and condescending. Some point to the scandals and corruption that have plagued the church and assume these incidents are typical—that if you scratch the veneer of Christianity, you find the same flaws, lusts, greed, and self-centeredness at the core of every person's life, whether they claim the name of Jesus or not. Many accuse church leaders of ulterior motives in maintaining a profitable business, an exclusive club, or a system of power. A popular quote often attributed to Gandhi makes this point: "I like your Christ. I do not like your Christians. Your Christians are so unlike your Christ."[2] All of these objections come down to one common element: the lack of real change in Christians' lives. The world can find plenty of evidence that many of us are not Christlike, and that evidence is magnified in the hands of those who reject our faith.

Think of the testimony we could have if those scandals, behavioral flaws, and mixed motives became rare exceptions rather than common observations and headlines. What impact would it have on our loved ones? Our society? Our governments, schools, media, and community organizations? What if Christians became widely known as desirable friends, employees, and volunteers because of our humility, servant-heartedness, integrity, and love? What if we presented a clear picture of Jesus and demonstrated the power of a transformed life in ways that only our most strident critics could deny? What if we radically changed the way people see Jesus and His followers? We might actually turn the world upside down (again), and God might draw many to faith through us.

> *What if Christians became widely known as desirable friends, employees, and volunteers because of our humility, servant-heartedness, integrity, and love?*

As it stands right now, believers can be as materialistic and greedy—and as deeply in debt—as nonbelievers. Disturbing numbers of Christians are trapped in pornography and other addictive behaviors. The divorce rate among committed Christians is substantially lower than that among non-Christians, but it is still alarmingly high. Those who claim the name of Christ know how to develop destructive habits, sabotage their relationships, and misdirect their priorities as well as anybody. But all of that can change. Transformed lives are contagious. We can become catalysts of change not only for Christian culture but for society as a whole.

Committed, discipled, transformed Christians are not perfect. If you are on that path of transformation, you know very well that we face many of the same kinds of struggles that everyone else faces, and sometimes we stumble, stagger, or fall. But we continue to grow because we recognize that Jesus owns our priorities, our time, our

Wherever you are on that spectrum from casual Christian to frustrated Christian to growing and changing Christian, you can learn the principles and tools of greater transformation.

money, our relationships, our families, and our own selves. We make it our goal to thrive in marriage or singleness, raise kids, serve others, seek purity, maintain integrity, and live His way rather than ours. We may not be perfect at it, but we are growing in that direction.

Wherever you are on that spectrum from casual Christian to frustrated Christian to growing and changing Christian, you can learn the principles and tools of greater transformation. The statistics, problems, and frustrations we've covered in this chapter do not have to be your story. We've introduced three hindrances to life-change—spiritual ignorance, spiritual isolation, and spiritual myopia—as common pitfalls for all of us. But it is important to know from the outset, without a doubt, that you are not stuck in any of them. Paul identified some profound, practical truths in the fourth chapter of Ephesians that can change your life. We will unpack them in ways that I think will be encouraging and empowering for you. Transformation really is possible, it is truly miraculous, and it is promised by the God who loves you and has designed you to reflect who He is.

Diagnostic Questions

- When you think about the possibility of genuine life transformation, what aspects of it excite you? Do any aspects of it frighten or intimidate you? If so, why?
- In which areas of your life have you been frustrated with lack of change? At this moment, how motivated are you to pursue change in those areas?
- What past teaching, experiences, and hopes are influencing your expectations for future transformation? How would you describe your expectations for change right now? Do you believe real, lasting change is possible? Why or why not?
- Which of the three inhibitors of change—spiritual ignorance, spiritual isolation, and spiritual myopia—seem relevant to you? Why?

CHAPTER 2

Are You Living
For God's Approval or
From God's Approval?

The Pevensie children were not much different from other kids their age, but when they discovered a portal into another kingdom—through a wardrobe in an old professor's house—they began to discover an entirely new identity. In three volumes of C. S. Lewis's *Chronicles of Narnia,* they went back and forth between their normal lives in one realm—the world as we know it—and their lives as royalty in another realm, the world of Narnia. As they grew to understand their new identity, they grew into their responsibilities. Their bearing and attitudes changed. They realized they were made for more than the lives they once knew in war-torn England. They became who they were called to be.

Themes of royalty in disguise and discovering a new and true identity are common in old fairy tales and today's fantasy fiction. We call them "Cinderella" and "rags-to-riches" stories because we only need a word or two to identity the hopes and longings within them. We love stories of humble people being elevated to privileged positions, of the destitute having their dreams come true, and of transformations from "sick and tired" to "happily ever after." These themes seem to be written into our psyche—almost as if we're drawn to them by design.

Perhaps we are. In a very real sense, that's the story of our redemption and restoration into the image of God. We were dead in our trespasses and sins but have been raised to new life and are now seated with Christ in heavenly places (Eph. 2:1–10). We were once "not a people," but now we are a chosen people, a royal priesthood, a holy nation, God's own special possession brought out of darkness and into the light (1 Peter 2:9–10). We were worthy of death and judgment, but we have been promised the privilege of reigning with Christ on earth (Rev. 5:10). We are new creations, designed to live out stories of miraculous transformation (2 Cor. 5:17). According to Scripture, this identity as new creations in Christ has already happened. Our nature has already radically changed.

The Christian life is the journey between the new identity we've already been given and entering into its fullness.

As we've seen, many Christians don't know who they are. Most of us don't begin with a clear vision of who we're called to be. Even if we know we are called to be like Christ, we spend years trying to figure out what that means. The Christian life is the journey between the new identity we've already been given and entering into its fullness. We are given a new name to use in prayer and faith, a new spiritual wardrobe to try on and grow into, new gifts to unpack and exercise, and a new kind of relationships in which we see people not in light of their past but in light of their future. And this radically new life is based entirely on our union with and identity in Christ.

That's why Paul begins so many of his letters with statements of identity. He calls the troublesome Corinthians "holy" and "sanctified," even though they weren't acting very holy or sanctified yet

(1 Cor. 1:2; 2 Cor. 1:1). In his letter to the Ephesians, he expanded that typical language into sweeping statements about his readers' chosenness, forgiveness, and adoption as God's children. Why? Because before we're ever told what to do as followers of Jesus, we need to know who we are in Him. Our behavior always flows from our sense of identity. When we know who we truly are, we see God, ourselves, and our world differently. And when we see differently, we live differently. We move in the direction of the vision God has given us.

So it's vital to cultivate that vision, to understand what Scripture says about you and live in light of that identity. If you don't believe you have been made righteous, you will never be able to live righteously. You may have noticed that. Like a commoner in a fairy tale finding out that he or she is really a prince or princess, you can learn from Scripture that you aren't the failure you might have thought you were. You aren't permanently stuck in any of the problems that seem to keep you down, even when you feel as if you are. You aren't a "sinner" anymore, even if you sin sometimes; the New Testament doesn't use that term for those who have been redeemed.[3] Along with all who believe, you are a saint, holy and beloved, a child of the living God, adopted into the royal family, with His whole kingdom in front of you.

That's why it is vital to put aside your old, false identities. Whether you recognize them or not, you have them. Everyone does. But they will not help you going forward. You'll need to be able to see yourself as God sees you, to actually believe what the Bible says about you, and carry the hope and promise He has for you throughout your journey of metamorphosis.

This has nothing to do with putting more weight on your shoulders. Your metamorphosis will not burn you out, frustrate you, or fatigue you. It actually takes the weight off you and hands it to the

Holy Spirit. It unveils the real you, the identity God has given you in your new nature. Like the Pevensie children, you begin to see yourself and your world in a completely new way. As you do, you will grow into the privileges and responsibilities you've been given.

What Do Those Promises Really Tell Us?

I have a friend who is extraordinarily gifted and appeared to be doing all the right things, but he struggled with temptation, failure, guilt, and self-condemnation for years, even as a pastor and missionary. He beat himself up constantly for not living up to his calling. But all of his prayers and Bible study, all of his efforts at self-discipline, and all of his inner rebukes never brought about the change he longed for. Sometimes he would experience victory over sin for long periods of time, and to most people, he looked like a pretty godly person. But one lapse would lead to more inward guilt and condemnation, which magnified his sense of failure, and the cycle would start all over again. He was living from his old identity, even as a new creation.

Part of my friend's problem was his deep desire to live for God's approval—to become a son in whom the Father was well pleased. Eventually it dawned on him that the message of the gospel is that we are already accepted as God's children by faith and he had nothing more to prove. He also realized that his extreme focus on his own sin and his identity as a sinner was unbiblical. Scripture is clear that our sin has been paid for by Christ, our debts have been canceled, and our offenses are removed from us as far as the east is from the west, and to keep focusing on them puts us at odds with God's Word. Only when he came to see himself as a new creation—and really began to believe his identity as a completely forgiven, beloved son of God, united with Jesus—did change begin to happen. His transformation began with a new perspective in the depths of his heart.

God promises us more than superficial, cosmetic changes. The Bible is not a book of advice on how to become a little different, be a little better, and grow a little more. It doesn't encourage us just to have greater willpower, stronger disciplines, and deeper motives. It gives us an entirely new source of life, casts a new vision, and calls us into new experiences. It really does speak to us as new creations.

That's one of the reasons so many people are frustrated with their lack of change. Biblical promises are so enormous, and when people seem to fall so short of them, they are left in that gap wondering what went wrong. But the promises about transformation and our new identity are clear. When you are in Christ, you can expect certain things to happen on the inside that will eventually work their way outward into every area of your life. It's a process, and it takes time. It isn't automatic, and it isn't easy. But the living, resurrected Jesus really is inside you, and when you learn to participate with Him, things will indeed change.

When that happens, you'll know it's the grace of God operating in you and not just something you manufactured on our own. You may not recognize it in the moment—you probably won't hear choirs of angels or peals of thunder with every dramatic shift in your life—but when you look back over time, you'll be amazed at the difference.

You may also be surprised at the kind of difference God brings about in you. The holy transformation promised in Scripture is not about becoming more religious, exerting more willpower, reading the Bible and praying for longer periods of time, or just changing your habits. Those kinds of changes are wonderful, and they may be byproducts of your transformation, but the new creation is not primarily about developing a strong will and behavioral

The new you is supernatural, not your best version of the old you.

disciplines. More likely, you will find a new compassion and patience growing inside you, a desire to help people at their point of need, or a growing ambition to serve God in creative or influential ways. You won't be immune to discouragement or frustration, but you'll draw new strength from a deeper source. The Holy Spirit will shape your thoughts, feelings, and actions because He has taken up residence within you and you are learning to let Him lead. The new you is supernatural, not your best version of the old you.

Allow me to paint a few word pictures to describe the kind of change we're talking about.

Picture #1

Imagine coming home after an exhausting and stressful day. You close the door to the world and lean against it for a moment. It's time to unwind. But a buzz on your phone lets you know a message is waiting. You listen as you kick off your shoes.

You hear the tension in the voice before you even recognize whose it is. Tom, a not-so-close friend, needs help and called you. But instead of a sense of imposition, your focus immediately shifts away from yourself and your difficult day. Compassion for Tom and renewed energy seem to flow from nowhere. You find yourself helping out, even changing a life that evening. You arrive back at home outwardly exhausted, but inwardly refreshed. There's no human explanation for the depth of your love and compassion. You are nearly as amazed by your response as Tom was. In a matter of a few hours, you both experienced and gave supernatural, unconditional love.

Picture #2

You hear of an astonishing windfall only to realize that the recipient of this good fortune is someone who has wronged you in the past. This person who deeply hurt you has cashed in on life's lottery.

But imagine a surprising reaction: joy and gratitude for God's blessing on this person. It goes beyond realizing that you *should* respond that way. You really are happy for them. An overwhelming sense of peace fills your soul, confirming that the long road of forgiving and blessing them in obedience to Romans 12:14–21 has finally come to an end.

A close friend observes your reaction, questions your sanity, and wants to know how you can possibly be happy for someone who has treated you so badly.

Picture #3

This one will take more imagination. As the result of an unexpected development—your death—you suddenly find yourself able to hear the honest conversations of your children and closest friends as they gather at your home after your funeral. They describe you as one of the most patient, faithful, Christlike people they have ever known. These aren't the common platitudes or exaggerations people tend to say after funerals. These are heartfelt comments about you actually having become the kind of person we all long to become—loving and strong. They describe your joy, accepting attitude, and fun-loving outlook. They express tearful appreciation for your integrity, faithfulness to God, and loyalty to people. They talk about your heart, your warmth, and your passion for both the lovely and the unlovely of this world. Can you imagine realizing that your life was so changed, so transformed, that you were a little mirror of Christ? Your life was so dominated by God's Spirit that you authentically reflected His presence. Can you imagine that?

Can Imagination Become Reality?

This kind of supernatural transformation is not the stuff of saints and superstars. It's real, it's powerful, and it's available to every person in whom His Spirit dwells. My hope is for these mental images to awaken a deep longing in you. These pictures are possible. God's Word outlines a game plan for what I just described actually happening in your life. Christ actually being formed in you is achievable. In fact, it's God's will for every person.

You can't fake these reactions and testimonies. They go way beyond behavior modification. Did you notice what was missing? There was no mention of cleaning up your morality, curbing your language, or changing a few inward attitudes. Nobody talked about giving a little money to charity, going to church more often, or setting records for prayer and Bible reading. All of those are important and valuable, but they are outcomes of spiritual transformation, not the essence of it. They don't produce our inward change; they flow from it. What I'm describing is not something that someone can do through mere discipline, no matter how committed they are. I'm talking about something that's supernatural—inside-out change. You can't invent godly compassion. You can't fake an attitude of gratitude that comes to your mind when someone who has deeply wounded you is blessed. Those responses mean something has happened in your heart.

That's what God's promises tell us. And the promise of this book is to lead you through the God-inspired teaching of the early church, specifically the words of Paul in his letter to the Ephesians. Early Christian teaching, and the changed lives of early Christians, moved an ordinary group of people from various backgrounds— rich, poor, men, women, slaves, and outcasts, many of whom were former idol worshipers—to turn their world upside down. They not only experienced transformation; they caused it in their society. People recognized them as being like Jesus.

This is not a spiritual secret or some hidden mystery. It's not pie-in-the-sky teaching that will get your hopes up but leave you disappointed in the end. It has been test-driven for two thousand years, and I've witnessed this transformation in my ministry and in the lives of many others. When the biblical truths in this book are applied, remarkable changes happen. I've heard the testimonies and read the letters. I've seen it at work in small groups and individual lives of men and women, young and old, across social, economic, and cultural backgrounds. I've seen enough to know that God is in the business of real spiritual transformation.

What Does a Changed Life Look Like?

The degree to which digital images can be manipulated today provides plenty of graphic pictures of transformation. Movies are full of them—characters can morph from humans to animals and back again, or from normal people to superheroes with special powers, or from aliens to humanoid figures and back again. Scenes shift from one geographic location to another with a quick manipulation of the background. We have no trouble envisioning radical change today because it is represented so frequently and impressively in film, advertisements, and art.

This is not a new phenomenon, of course. Everyone is familiar with before-and-after pictures. They are a great inspiration for physical regimens, remodeling proposals, and product sales. And nature provides its own examples: the stages of life, a change of seasons, the process between planting and harvest, the metamorphosis of a caterpillar into a butterfly. The possibility of transformation is put in front of us constantly.

The word "morph" comes from the Greek *morphe*. It refers to the unique form or nature of a person or thing. It is used in the New Testament for Jesus, "who, being in very *nature* God . . . made himself nothing by taking the very *nature* of a servant" (Phil. 2:6–7, emphasis added). The verb *morpho'o* refers to an inward form or essence rather than an external shape. That essence generally can't be changed without some divine work involved, as in Paul's sense of being in childbirth "until Christ is *formed* in you" (Gal. 4:19, emphasis added). Paul seems to be suggesting a fundamental transformation of human nature.

Paul gets more specific about that in his letter to the Romans, when he tells them no longer to conform "to the pattern of this world, but be transformed by the renewing of your mind" (Rom. 12:2). The word translated as "transformed" is the Greek *metamorphoó*, a compound of the verb that you probably recognize as the origin of our English word "metamorphosis." Paul is literally telling his readers to undergo a morphing that reshapes them from the pattern or mold of the surrounding world into the likeness of Jesus. The concept expressed in this word gives us a key for understanding how spiritual transformation occurs.

Willpower Christianity leads to frustration and disappointment. Spiritual metamorphosis empowered by God leads to genuine, supernatural, satisfying change.

Nowhere does it imply trying harder to be holy or do better. It calls us to participate in God's power to transform us, to partner with Him in the process of change. Willpower Christianity leads to frustration and disappointment. Spiritual metamorphosis empowered by God leads to genuine, supernatural, satisfying change.

Sounds drastic, doesn't it? But that's the point. The experience of change may seem incremental and slow at times, but it is based on a radical change that has already occurred in our participation in the death and resurrection of Jesus. Just as God created the world in the beginning, He re-creates us in a new genesis when we enter into the life of Jesus by faith. That's why Paul can say all things are new. We are a new creation in Christ.

Maybe you've longed for a metamorphosis—a different identity, a "makeover," a new start, a new phase of life in a different place or with a different job or circle of friends. Maybe you've wondered what it's like to "morph" like a character in a science-fiction or superhero movie. Those are symptoms of a genuine, God-given desire, and Scripture says that a real, lasting version of that metamorphosis is possible. You can enter into it by faith.

Jesus implied this concept of metamorphosis when He said, "I have come that they may have life, and that they may have it more abundantly" (John 10:10 NKJV). We have life, but there are degrees of it, just as a caterpillar is alive, but not quite in the same way a butterfly is. The later stage is "more abundant," the fullness of what a creation is to become. God doesn't want to leave us where we are. He wants to bring us all the way into fullness.

Because we were created in God's image, that's our ultimate design. But as we have all experienced, the image of God in us was shattered in the fall, when sin entered the world. It's still there, but it needs repair, and a little fixing up isn't enough. There's no way to mend the broken pieces any more than we could put an eggshell or a broken window back together and make it look just the same. We need a new birth, a regenesis, a creative act that supernaturally fixes the unfixable. So God sent Jesus, the exact representation of His nature (Heb. 1:3), and made it possible to put His Spirit within us. We are now being transformed by grace through faith into the image of Jesus, who is the image of God, and therefore are becoming the image of God again (Rom. 8:29).

The moment we came to Christ, we were saved, forgiven, and born of God's Spirit. God's plan from that moment forward is to use every circumstance, relationship, problem, pain, joy, and opportunity to conform us into the likeness of Jesus. But that's not only

We long for something more because we were designed for something more.

His plan; it's also our longing, which explains why so many stories, movies, self-help programs, dreams, and desires are filled with images of new identities, transformed lives, and satisfying ends. We long for something more because we were designed for something more. And the only way for that longing to be fulfilled is to recapture the image of God that was once in us and is now broken.

That longing shows up in a lot of different ways, but they all involve getting better and being different. No one longs to be a worse parent or a substandard employee. No couple looks into each other's eyes and says, "I know we have a really good marriage, but I'd like to work on communicating less and drifting apart so we can get divorced in a few years." No one dreams of mediocrity. The human heart will always try to fill itself with something—possessions, positions, or people—even though our self-designed strategies are ultimately unhealthy and unsatisfying. But even those unhealthy, unsatisfying strategies are based on real needs and desires. Something inside us craves positive change in almost everything we do.

Real fulfillment of our deepest desires comes in the context of a growing relationship with God and alignment with His will for our lives. So often the emphasis in Romans 12:2 is so strongly focused on the command not to be conformed to this world that we forget the second half of the passage: to "be transformed by the renewing of your mind" that you may "test" what the will of God is—"good, pleasing, and perfect." The promises and instructions of Scripture always point us to His goodness. The centerpiece of His will for us is Christlikeness—being filled with the Spirit of Jesus and transforming into His nature. That's the metamorphosis God offers us.

The Process of Transformation

Transformation takes time, but it is written into our spiritual DNA when we place our faith in Jesus. Paul told the Philippians that God was at work within them "both to desire and to work for His good pleasure" (Phil. 2:13 NASB). He keeps turning us in that direction, no matter how many times we struggle or fall. Metamorphosis occurs over the course of our lives as Christians in three major stages. These aren't perfectly linear; periods of growth can overlap, and we may find ourselves circling through the second and third stages again and again. But God has designed us to grow, by grace through faith, in these three phases:

- **Spiritual birth**—When we receive Jesus by faith as our Savior, we are born again. That's the initial stage (John 3:1–16; 2 Cor. 5:17). Our sins are forgiven, we are justified in God's sight, the Holy Spirit resides within us, we become part of the family of God, and the growth process begins.
- **Spiritual maturity**—The growth process leads to spiritual maturity (Phil. 1:6; Col. 2:6–7). This is the heart of our transformation process, when we begin to reflect the person and character of Christ. The fruit of the Holy Spirit grows in us, producing love, joy, peace, patience, kindness, goodness, faithfulness, gentleness, and self-control (Gal. 5:22–23 NASB). Our attitudes, words, actions, and relationships take on a Christlike tone.
- **Spiritual reproduction**—As we grow, we turn outward and serve others. We become part of the disciple-making process (Matt. 28:19–20; 2 Tim. 2:2). Just as humans and animals become biologically mature enough to reproduce, the works of God in us are reproduced in the lives of others as we spiritually mature. That doesn't mean we can't lead people to Christ and help make disciples immediately—many people do—but we

generally minister to others according to the maturity God has worked in us. He uses us in the process of birthing and growing other believers.

These stages of transformation can play out in a wide variety of ways. Just as no two people's physical or intellectual growth is exactly the same, no two people's spiritual growth follows the exact same trajectory. In other words, it is rarely helpful to compare ourselves with others. We can learn from others' experiences, but every life follows somewhat different directions, paces, and processes. The means of change are remarkably consistent—God has told us how change happens—but we can apply them to an unlimited variety of circumstances and timelines.

For example, Geoff came from a broken home. His father was absent, and his mother was an alcoholic who attempted suicide several times during his childhood. From high school into his early thirties, Geoff experimented with alcohol, drugs, cults, and relationships that inevitably ended up broken. He made rash and unwise business decisions, tempering any success with unnecessary and unprofitable risks. His kidneys began to fail, he declared bankruptcy, and his life seemed hopeless and wasted.

But Geoff met a man named Will who cared for him, prayed with him, and brought help and hope to his life. Will introduced Geoff to other Christians, and for the first time, Geoff felt loved and accepted. He realized they had characteristics he didn't have, and through the testimony of their lives, he eventually accepted Christ. He experienced the joy and peace he had never known. His troubles didn't disappear, but his life began to change. And with the help of Will and his friends, and with continual exposure to worship, fellowship, teaching, and God's Word, Geoff experienced a new kind of life.

No one gave Geoff a set of rules to follow, but as he grew, he discovered new desires to live God's way and reject whatever didn't fit God's will. His craving for drugs and alcohol diminished. He avoided relationships that would put him in tempting or troubling situations. His work ethic, sense of integrity, and use of money and time changed in keeping with his new priorities. It took him almost four years to get his finances in order, he faced many health and relational issues, and he didn't become sinless. He had setbacks, challenges, and questions. But he also knew he had a means of outgrowing sin and overcoming problems, being held accountable in loving and accepting relationships, and learning new ways. He persisted in faith and grew increasingly mature.

Eventually, Geoff became a "Will" for other people, giving to others what Will had given him. He feels godly compassion for men with experiences and lifestyles similar to those in his past. He is a clear example of each stage of transformation—birth, growth, and fruitfulness. We love dramatic testimonies like Geoff's because they demonstrate the gospel and its power to change lives. I've known people who wish they had such a powerful testimony, forgetting the cost and the pain that went into it. But even though it is not necessarily typical, it is certainly normal. It's how God often works.

Geoff knows his transformation came from God. Geoff may have been involved in every decision every step of the way, but the desires behind those decisions and the fruitfulness that came from them were the outworking of God's grace and power. Change happened not because Geoff was smarter or more loved than others but because he came to know and understand his new identity in Christ and cooperate early in his Christian life with how God works in the transformation process.

Unlike Geoff, Beth grew up in a Christian home and regularly attended church with her family. She had heard the Bible preached all of her life, accepted Christ in her early teenage years, enjoyed youth group activities, and stayed in touch with her Christian friends when she went away to college. She spent a few years questioning and exploring her faith, but she never really forgot her roots. But even though she had always identified herself as a Christian and had genuinely believed in Jesus, she had never really learned how to apply God's Word in a way that would produce growth. She finished college, embarked on a rewarding career, got married, moved to a new city, and drifted away from God. She was saved by God's grace but lived out her faith sometimes on Sundays. And over time, those Sundays became fewer and further between.

That changed after Beth and her husband had their first child. They wanted to bring their son up in a Christian home and started going to a church in the city where they had recently moved. Beth found herself needing help in many areas of life—marriage, motherhood, postpartum depression, putting her career on hold, and trying to make friends in an unfamiliar city. She became desperate to recapture the truth she had once known, and God's Word became more and more relevant to her life.

Beth joined a small group at her church and observed other women applying Scripture to real-life situations, sharing their struggles, praying for each other faithfully, and demonstrating the love and fellowship she was longing for. They warmly accepted her, encouraged her, and helped her apply God's Word not only to her situations but, more importantly, to her heart. They also worked together in community outreach, providing practical assistance to single mothers in a low-income neighborhood. Beth began to feel fulfilled in a way she had never known—and eventually became the leader of a small group that ministered to people in situations similar to hers.

Kyle came from the same background Beth did—the same church, in fact—but never really experienced his family's faith as anything other than a part of their social life. He didn't accept

Christ until he got involved with a campus ministry in college, and at first his whole world seemed new. Scripture suddenly made sense. He craved fellowship with other believers. His desires completely changed, and so did his major. He wanted to go into full-time ministry. He thought he had found his calling.

After a couple of years, Kyle realized that he wasn't living up to his calling, no matter how much he tried. Like Bobby in the introduction, and like me at one point early in my Christian walk, he felt like giving up. And he might have, if his roommates in his senior year hadn't helped him understand what was going on in his heart. They shared their struggles with him and talked about how they were overcoming them. They modeled compassion, grace, and patience. They showed him what God's acceptance looks like, and they valued his gifts and insights as reflections of God's calling for his life. They helped him see himself in a new way.

Over time, Kyle stopped feeling like a failure, even though he still failed at times. He learned how to receive grace and forgiveness, grow in his relationships with other believers, and exercise his spiritual gifts for others just as he benefited from theirs. Once again, his whole world seemed new. He felt like he belonged, and he wanted nothing more than to help other struggling believers feel like they belonged too.

These stories illustrate some of the different circumstances and timelines by which Christians are transformed. They reflect a variety of experiences. But you probably noticed the three phases of growth in each of them. And if you look back over your past, you will likely discern them in your life too.

Where do you fit into these phases of transformation? Which ones have you experienced, which characteristics are growing stronger, and where do you see your need for greater change? How have you sensed the Spirit of Jesus at work within you, and what do you envision ahead? These are good questions to ask, not for the sake of self-criticism but for discerning where God is taking you from this point forward.

Transformation is for everyone, not just for some ideal, spiritually elite people who happen to "get it." The stories above are not about people keeping the rules and living up to idealized, romanticized versions of heroic Christians. They are about spiritual rebirth, a relationship, a new love, and then change that grows out of that love. This is not only possible. It's normal and expected, even commanded. It's not for "someday." It's for now. Yes, there are plenty of Christians around you who don't seem to grasp that, but you are not called to follow them. You are called to follow Jesus and the words His Spirit inspired in Scripture. This is an essential aspect of the Christian life, and it's for you.

Where Are You in This Process?

Growth is hard to quantify. Christlikeness is even harder, especially since measuring ourselves against Jesus always reveals that we are significantly short of the goal. But transformation is nevertheless noticeable. We recognize the difference between before-and-after pictures, between a caterpillar and a butterfly, or between a seed and a harvest. Transformation looks like people who have been lost, broken, or stuck becoming loved, healed, and free—and eager to offer what God has given them to others.

Where are you on the path of transformation? The following diagnostic tool will help you assess where you are—again, not in order to get lost in introspection, lament your lack of change, or make you feel like a failure, but to get a clear idea of where you're going from here. It will give you some perspective on your transformation into the image of Christ and, I hope, be an encouragement one day when you look back and see how far you've come.

Rank yourself (or better yet, ask a friend to help rank you) on the scale from 0 percent to 100 percent in the following areas. Don't worry if you don't fully understand the reason for or implications of these statements now. They will be explained in more detail in our study of Ephesians 4. To the best of your knowledge,

1 I am currently involved in activities and training that are equipping me to do the work of the ministry.

Never	Rarely	Sporadically	Consistently
0%	10–15%	50–60%	90–100%

2 I am regularly participating in intentional, meaningful, biblical worship.

Never	Rarely	Sporadically	Consistently
0%	10–15%	50–60%	90–100%

3 I am currently in an apprentice or mentoring relationship with an older believer who is stimulating my spiritual growth.

Never	Rarely	Sporadically	Consistently
0%	10–15%	50–60%	90–100%

4 I am currently ministering and building into the lives of others.

Never	Rarely	Sporadically	Consistently
0%	10–15%	50–60%	90–100%

5 I am becoming more like Christ, as evidenced by a desire to read God's Word, a disciplined study and understanding of His Word, and an ability to see through false teaching.

Never	Rarely	Sporadically	Consistently
0%	10–15%	50–60%	90–100%

6 I am becoming more like Christ, as evidenced by enjoying one or more deep, authentic Christ-centered relationships.

Not currently	1–2	3 or more
0%	50–60%	90–100%

7 I am currently in a small group where speaking the truth in love is common. I have three or four gut-level accountability relationships that are helping me through the most sensitive areas of my life.

Not currently	Hit and miss	Yes
0%	50–60%	90–100%

8 I am becoming more like Christ, as evidenced by a desire to become more deeply involved with God's people, to worship, to learn, to serve, and to meet the needs of others. I have a clear sense that I fit in the body of Christ. I am loved by others, and I find myself caring and helping them in increasing measure.

Never	Rarely	Significantly	Yes
0%	10–15%	50–60%	90–100%

9 I am becoming more like Christ, as evidenced by compassion for and acts of service on behalf of "the least of these" (Matt. 25:40, 45)—those who need provision of food, clothing, shelter, and other acts of mercy.

Never	Rarely	Significantly	Yes
0%	10–15%	50–60%	90–100%

10 I am following Jesus' Great Commission by sharing God's love verbally and as a lifestyle to make disciples and witness to the gospel (Matt 28:19–20).

Never	Rarely	Significantly	Yes
0%	10–15%	50–60%	90–100%

Are you beginning to see where you are in the transforming process? Are you growing in love? Being grounded in Scripture? Ministering to others? These are not the only indicators of growth—the nature and character of Jesus is multifaceted—but they are identified in Paul's instructions to the Ephesians and good markers of change. God has made provision for all of these things to happen when we place ourselves under His leadership, envision the identity and calling He has given us, and learn to participate in His mission in this world.

If you're like most followers of Jesus, you have seen yourself somewhere in the last two chapters and felt two emotions: (1) at least some degree of regret over a lack of change in your life, no matter how much you've already experienced; and (2) hopeful anticipation about what God is able to do in profoundly transforming your nature to be more like Him. And, as we've seen, it begins with your awareness of who He really is, who you really are, and what He really wants to do in your life.

My hope is that you are already beginning to see the new you— that you are sensing your true identity in Christ, getting a picture of the person God has called you to be, and eager to explore all the promises and possibilities of a radically new life. At the very least, I hope you now believe it's possible to put any frustrations about lack of transformation in the past and are eager to enter into a process of genuine, lasting change.

CHAPTER 3

Is a Changed Life Possible for *Everyone*?

EPHESIANS 4:1-6

D ave was addicted to pornography. He was also a believer in Jesus. He had been born again, yet he struggled with a sin that kept coming up again and again and seemed stronger than he was. If the people around Dave had known about his secret, many would have considered the contradictions in his life too great for him to be considered a Christian. Deep down, Dave often thought the exact same thing. The transformation other believers experienced seemed wonderful and exciting—but way out of his reach. It seemed like it just didn't apply to him.

Dave felt weighed down, always guilty, always tying every adversity and disappointment in life to God's judgment, even though he knew plenty of Bible verses about forgiveness and our debt of sin being canceled at the cross of Jesus. He knew he needed help, but for a long time, he was too ashamed to ask for it. But when he saw a notice about a support group for men with his problem at a church in another part of town, he decided to go. There he heard stories from men who had overcome their addiction and were living in freedom. He wanted that. He knew it might be a long road, but for the first time, he felt a glimmer of hope. Over time, hope grew, and Dave felt the joy of new life rising up within him. It was almost like being born again . . . again. He was experiencing a personal renaissance.

Societies go through renaissance and renewal too. Cultural and intellectual changes in northern Italy in the 1300s, for example, sparked a new interest in old things. Many scholars and artists began exploring the Greek and Roman past and trying to recapture its glories. Latin literature, Roman art and sculpture, classical philosophies and rhetoric, and beliefs about ancient governments stirred up new visions and ideals. The movement spread into many other parts of Europe throughout the next two centuries, and Western culture was transformed, so much so that later historians called it a rebirth—a Renaissance.

The Renaissance was a time of exploring ideas. To many of the scholars, philosophers, artists, and artisans living in that time, everything felt new. A new world was opening up before them—figuratively at first, and then literally after Columbus's voyages to the Americas—and imaginations soared. But the sense of newness was really a rediscovery of old roots, a return to origins, a search for foundations in history and in the created universe. Many intellectuals sought answers to fundamental questions about God's design and our purposes and potential as human beings. They wanted to understand the nature of things and how life was meant to be.

When we place our faith in Jesus, we undergo a spiritual rebirth and enter into a new kingdom with a new culture. In our renaissance, everything changes—or at least has the potential to change. We look to the past for the image of God and our original design, things that were lost to us long ago and are now being restored. We reconnect with our created purpose and embrace a very new and more foundational way of life. Once made in the image of God, we are being restored into the character and nature of Jesus, the perfect image of God. Literally and figuratively, we are reborn. And every believer is given the calling and the supernatural power to live out this rebirth as new creations. Renaissance is for *everyone*.

Your Calling

That's where Paul begins in his teaching in Ephesians 4—with that balance between new and old. The context of this section of the letter is important. Paul has spent the first three chapters establishing our new identity, emphasizing that we have been chosen, adopted into God's family, and united with Christ. We were once dead in our trespasses and sins and are now seated with Christ above all other spiritual powers (2:1, 6). It's the ultimate rags-to-riches story.

As these first three chapters come to a close, Paul prays a profound prayer about being rooted and grounded in the love of Christ (3:16–19)—the foundational position for our entire lives and the basis for any change that will come—and then praises the God who is able to do immeasurably more than we can ask or imagine. How does God do that? The answer offers a key to our entire transformation as new creations: "according to his power that is at work within us" (3:20).

That's a huge statement, and it's why the change you long for is not a burden to bear. It's your responsibility, but God provides the power. Your position in Christ, your foundation in the height, width, length, and depth of His love, and the working of His Spirit within you flow from an immeasurable power that results in God's glory. You may *feel* trapped in sin, guilt, and shame, but you aren't. Corporately and individually, you are part of a renaissance of epic proportions.

That's the truth Paul has just covered as Ephesians 4 opens. We are called to a completely new way of life, but that new way is built on timeless foundations and original design. We are to live in a way that is worthy of the sweeping, sovereign purposes of God's kingdom we have entered into as believers.

> As a prisoner for the Lord, then, I urge you to live a life worthy of the calling you have received. Be completely humble and gentle; be patient, bearing with one another in love. Make every effort to keep the unity of the Spirit through the bond of peace. There is one body and one Spirit, just as you were called to one hope when you were called; one Lord, one faith, one baptism; one God and Father of all, who is over all and through all and in all. (Eph. 4:1–6)

Your calling is to let Jesus live His life in you and through you. He is both the exact image of God and the perfect template of humanity, so when you allow His Spirit to work in your heart, you are being transformed into the new life you have been given, which also aligns with the original image you were created to carry. If you've ever wondered what God has called you to do in life, this transformation is where it begins. Before all other callings, this is the renaissance that will shape the rest of your existence throughout eternity.

Your calling is to let Jesus live His life in you and through you.

Let's examine that calling more closely. The instruction "to live a life worthy of the calling you have received" is literally "to walk worthy of the calling by which you were called." That call is Jesus' invitation to enter into a relationship with Him. As Paul emphasized in the opening of this letter, you have been chosen, forgiven, adopted into God's family, sealed with His Spirit, and given an inheritance that lasts forever (Eph. 1:3–14). All the qualities Paul describes in the first three chapters of this letter, all of the spiritual blessings you have been given, all of the extravagant expressions of your relationship with Jesus and God's purposes for your life, are yours—forever. In light of everything that God has done and the new identity you now have in Him, Paul now turns to what you are to do: live a life that matches who you are.

That's really the summary of the whole chapter. The first three chapters have laid the foundation, as if to say, "Here are your new legs." Chapter 4 says, "Now walk with them." Of course, learning to walk is a process. It begins with the ability to stand upright, which can be quite a challenge for new legs. Then, with Mom and Dad cheering their little one on, she shifts weight from one foot to the other and takes her first step. It's wobbly, she tries to catch herself, and she will probably fall. She may even fall several times before successfully completing that first step. Nobody blames her. This is how it works. She will soon get her balance and be walking across the room.

Your transformation begins the same way. A whole new world lies open in front of you, but those first steps may be wobbly, and you'll have to risk falling again and again. But over time, you begin to walk like Jesus as a lifestyle. Your Father is cheering you on. You take one step of faith followed by another and then another. Sometimes those steps will take you out of your comfort zone, and you may lose your balance at times, but that's how it works. You begin to walk like Jesus by letting go of your old props and taking those first steps.

Paul uses a powerful word to describe this walk: "worthy." The Greek *axios* (from which we get "axis") refers to measuring weight by using a counterbalance, much like a teeter-totter. An item is placed on one end of the beam, and then weight is added to the other end until it becomes equal, or "worthy," and balances the scales. Paul is urging the Ephesian Christians, in light of their true, new identity, to make sure their behavior matches their beliefs. He has already reminded them of who they are. Now he calls them to level the beam, to make sure their outward lives line up with their inner identity. They need to live like the children of God, members of the royal family and the holy priesthood that they are.

Notice that this is not just a suggestion. Paul reminds the Ephesians that he is a prisoner for God's sake, and he uses strong language to urge them, implore them, even command them with the apostolic authority he has. It's a plea for every believer to be transformed inwardly and outwardly—to let Jesus live His life through us. God calls us to live out our faith in Christ with such consistency and integrity that it impacts our relationships, money, time, speech, and even our secret motives and thoughts.

The high standard of this calling—to bring our behavior in line with our new nature, which is like Jesus—trips up many Christians who are learning to walk. We came into this new kingdom culture by grace through faith, but as soon as we are told to "do" something, we revert to old ways of self-improvement. We start to base our relationship with God on performance. Many believers spend their entire lives subconsciously trying to earn God's favor because they forget that it has already been given. We try to become beloved children of God without realizing that we already are.

That's my story the first two or three years after becoming a Christian. I knew I was forgiven, had experienced the Holy Spirit, and believed He had taken up residence in my heart. I knew I was going to heaven. But I was still operating with serious misunderstandings about God and the gift of salvation. I somehow got the idea when I was young that God loves us when we're good but doesn't when we're bad,

A healthy spiritual life is not about trying really hard to be good or straining to be more disciplined in Bible reading and prayer.

and that idea carried over into my Christian life. But it's an unbiblical idea, terrible theology, and actually hinders being transformed by God's power.

God's unconditional love and grace are the basis of both our salvation *and* our transformation. A healthy spiritual life is not about trying really hard to be good or straining to be more disciplined in Bible reading and prayer. Genuine spiritual transformation is not measured by your attempts to clean up the outside of the cup (Matt. 23:25). Being really committed, giving some of your time or money to good causes, cleaning up your language, and keeping the "rules" of discipleship do not mean you've arrived at a place of spiritual maturity. They are byproducts of your walk with God, but when they become your focus, those efforts are merely religion—an attempt to meet God's standards with only human strength. They are an attempt to walk with God *for* your worth rather than walking with God *from* your worth. That's not the Christian life.

At its heart, the Christian life is realizing you were once dead but are now alive. Jesus lives in you, and all of His spiritual blessings, power, love, wisdom, inheritance, and character traits are already available to you. You'll need to learn to walk in them, but you don't have to acquire them. You live in what you've been given. You let the identity God has given you play out in daily life. Living this way is not an option; it's a command. The core of the Christian life is letting your relationship with Christ manifest inwardly and outwardly in all its fullness. That's your calling.

Practice Sacrificial, Others-Centered Relationships

How does that calling work? How do you really let Jesus' power and His character and blessings play out in your life? That's where Paul heads next.

This isn't a to-do list. It's a to-be list. Verses 2 and 3 of Ephesians

4 tell us to "be completely humble and gentle; be patient, bearing with one another in love. Make every effort to keep the unity of the Spirit through the bond of peace." God's teaching about life-change does not begin with a list of activities but with our attitudes and relationships. Four key words in this passage—humble, gentle, patient, and bearing—are grace-filled, Christlike attributes. They are essential components of our transformation into His image. We simply cannot be like Christ without these attitudes. They are integral to His nature.

The one expression of "doing" in this passage is "make every effort," and it's still about an attitude rather than an agenda. It's one word in the original language, and it describes eagerly, zealously, and diligently taking an action or developing a practice. But it's applied to the context of relationships. If we really want transformation, it will require us to make significant effort to do life in community with other believers.

Just as the Renaissance developed in a certain social environment, we change in relationships with other Christians. They form a "cocoon" of nurture and growth. Ideally, we are sheltered in a fellowship where our struggles can play out with grace, encouragement, and accountability. I realize many Christian fellowships over the centuries have not cheered on the first steps and stumbles of others and have not provided the safety for struggles to produce growth. But this kind of fellowship really does exist, and it's essential for genuine transformation.

> **God changes lives through the power of His Word and His Spirit in the context of sacrificial, others-centered relationships.**

Many Americans (and human beings in general) have an independent streak, that John Wayne–mentality of doing things ourselves. Many of us prefer Lone Ranger lifestyles or the idea of pulling ourselves up by our own bootstraps. But individualism can be destructive in our relationship with Jesus. The idea that it's just us, our Bible, and our prayers alone with God is never presented in the New Testament as normal. Our individualism places us outside of the nest where we are fed, taught, and protected.

Living in community with other believers is not optional. The Bible teaches us that God changes lives through the power of His Word and His Spirit in the context of sacrificial, others-centered relationships. A believer who is not in deep, intentional, authentic relationships with other believers in some kind of small group is probably a believer who isn't growing, no matter how many church services or ministry activities that person engages in. If a small group—a family, a ministry team, an accountability group, a Bible study—meets regularly, learns Scripture, and shares what God is teaching each member, speaking truth into each other's lives, change will occur. Lives can and will be supernaturally transformed by God's grace to be more loving and holy from the inside out in that kind of environment. That's the soil that produces growth.

The four attitudes Paul mentions in these verses involve other people. You can't be humble, gentle, or bearing with one another alone. You can be patient about events and processes, but patience is most often applied in our relationships with others. None of these attitudes are developed in a vacuum. They require community. Just as the Father, the Son, and the Holy Spirit live in a fellowship of perfect love, we become godly and Christlike when we grow toward perfect love in our relationships. Fellowship is like a spiritual petri dish for transformation.

Creating a Climate for Life-Change

If relationships are a necessary environment for transformation, and these four key attributes are central to our relationships, they are worth exploring a little deeper. We have entered into a new kingdom culture, a renaissance of God's purposes in our hearts and minds, and this is the start of what it looks like. These four attributes are fundamental values in our new lives.

Humility

Humility is often misunderstood. It means to have an accurate view of oneself—neither too high nor too low, but appropriate. Being humble does not mean we need to feel bad about ourselves, underestimate our value, or think of ourselves as small and unimportant. In fact, it means we don't really think about ourselves at all. Or, as is often said, "humility is not thinking less of yourself; it is thinking of yourself less."[4]

Paul spelled this out in Romans 12:3: "Do not think of yourself more highly than you ought, but rather think of yourself with sober judgment, in accordance with the faith God has distributed to each of you." At times, that may look like valuing others even more than ourselves (Phil. 2:3), but it's really an act of treating everyone—including yourself—with the value God places on each person. We recognize everyone's strengths and weaknesses, value what each member of the fellowship brings to the table, and focus on others more than ourselves. We walk with God not only from our own worth but in awareness of theirs.

> **Transformation requires sacrificial, others-centered relationships.**

Some forms of pride are obvious and easily rejected; others are more subtle and have become acceptable in Christian circles. People who talk about themselves and their problems all the time—not just to ask for prayer or help but to magnify their victimhood—are focused on themselves. That's pride, and it inhibits genuine fellowship and growth.

Transformation requires sacrificial, others-centered relationships. It involves servanthood. Humility is a focus, not a feeling, and it turns our attention toward others' needs. Jesus demonstrated this humble servanthood the night before His crucifixion when He took off His outer garment, wrapped a towel around His waist, and washed His disciples' feet (John 13:1–17). Paul echoed it in Philippians 2:5–11 when he wrote of Jesus voluntarily limiting His attributes and taking the form of a servant. When we put others first, we are becoming like Christ.

When you make a conscious effort to serve others in love, just as Jesus demonstrated, you will find Him manifesting His life and power through you. Don't be surprised if you also discover some un-Christlike attitudes coming up too; servanthood goes against our natural instincts. That's a great opportunity to let Christ work and practice the next attitude Paul mentions.

Gentleness

Gentleness means "to be considerate." It implies restraint, not insisting on guarding your own rights in every situation but deferring to the rights and needs of others. For example, when you know someone is wrong and you have the right answer, gentleness makes you want to protect them rather than embarrass them. When you know it's your turn but someone else thinks it's theirs, it enables you to let them go first. It's power under control.

Only hours after Jesus washed His disciples' feet, He willingly allowed Himself to be arrested. He could have called legions of angels to the scene, but He gently resisted. When the chief priests brought charges against Him, He gave no answer to defend Himself (Matt. 26:59–63; 27:11–14). Jesus did not remain silent in front of His accusers out of weakness. He stood silent because He was gentle. He was strong, with nothing to prove and no one to impress.

That's the image we are called to conform to.

As you give up your need to be "right" in your relationships, you may discover a bruised ego lingering within you, just waiting for opportunities to remind someone of how much you really know or what you could have done. In other words, you may have an irresistible urge to point out that you are being humble and gentle so no one mistakes your strength for weakness. If so, turn back to your identity in Christ. Rest in the fact that you are already and forever secure, loved, valued, and significant. God will exalt the humble in His own time (James 4:10; 1 Peter 5:6), and you can trust Him to do so. You don't have to manage your own PR. In the meantime, this power under control will allow you to identify with and experience a small measure of Christ's sufferings. Deep in your heart, transformational work is happening.

Patience

Patience is vital in the midst of that deep transformational work. There may be times when you are humbler and gentler than the people around you, and it isn't easy to live on the short end of a relationship for long. Patience is the ability to remain steadfast in the midst of suffering. It helps us not be personally offended. The Greek word is *makrothymia*—literally, a lot of heat. It means you have a long fuse before you get angry.

If you think you're on your own to defend yourself, that kind of patience isn't possible. But you aren't. You are in Christ. No one's opinions or actions have the power to determine who you are and how you respond. People who get angry easily and are always on edge to defend their rights are usually insecure deep inside. They don't understand that if they are in Christ, they are already complete, accepted, loved, and secure. Our patience, on the other hand, is rooted in our realization that we don't need others' approval and have nothing to prove because God loves us, defends us, vindicates us, and proves our value in His timing.

Bearing

Bearing with one another literally means to put up with each other—quirks, failures, idiosyncrasies, annoying habits, and all. Even after applying humility, gentleness, and patience to our relationships, there will still be people who don't reciprocate. We are still called to put up with them, to bear one another's burdens in love (Gal. 6:2). Why? Because that's what Christ does for us. He went to the cross not because He loved everything about us but because He loved *us*—"while we were still sinners" (Rom. 5:8). If we understand who we are in Christ (Eph. 1–3) and let Him live His life through us, we will put up with a lot. Our transformation process will not just accelerate in the context of our relationships. It will depend on how we respond to them in love.

Make Every Effort

Letting Jesus live through us does not mean we need to pray for more of Him. We already have Him. His Spirit dwells within us. It's not about getting more of Him but about Him getting more of us. We strip away remnants of the old nature in order for His Spirit and our new identity to show through. And, according to Paul, we are to "make every effort" (v. 3) to do that.

That implies struggle. If it were easy, we wouldn't need to take pains, be diligent, be eager and zealous to pay a price for it. With our whole heart, we

> **It's not about getting more of Him but about Him getting more of us.**

say, "I'm going to learn to be a servant. I'm going to learn to be gentle and give up my rights as God directs. I'm going to learn to be patient and have a long fuse. I'm going to learn to bear with other people in love. I'm not going to hang around only with people I like and who make me feel good but will reach out to other kinds of people with whom I am uncomfortable, and I'm going to treat them as Jesus would treat them."

That may sound a lot like willpower Christianity, and if our transformation only came down to resolutions like this, that's what it would be. As you are probably well aware, efforts to change by willpower lead to moderate improvement at best, burnout and failure at worst. Again, we learn to strike that balance between God's work and our own. We do make an effort and persist in what we are called to be and do, but we have to trust that God will meet us there and blow wind in our sails, with His life rising up within us. We don't transform ourselves, and He doesn't do it for us without our partnership. We participate in the process He has empowered and laid out before us.

We can't experience transformation just by keeping rules and being more religious, but that doesn't mean it's automatic either. We can't just passively, inactively receive it. We enter into a relationship by grace through faith, and once we understand who we are in Christ, we choose to practice specific attitudes whether we feel like it or not. The more we are transformed, the more our obedience seems to come naturally. But even when it goes against our natural grain—and we discover often that it does, especially early in our lives as believers—we still have to "make every effort." Transformation happens inside as we cooperate with God's Spirit to apply His character on the outside.

Many Christians are looking for a major encounter or emotional experience with God that will transform them immediately, much as Paul had on the Damascus road when Jesus appeared to him. We can be grateful for mountaintop experiences and how they serve as catalysts in our lives. But real change comes through the daily application of objective truth in real-life relationships. Through our conscious, willful obedience to the four attitudes above, the Holy Spirit begins to form the character and nature of Jesus within us. It's our responsibility to cultivate them, to put ourselves in position to develop and exercise them. It's God's responsibility to fill them with His life and power, giving us what we need as we need it.

What are we to "make every effort" to do, specifically? We are "to keep the unity of the Spirit through the bond of peace." We don't strive to achieve unity. The body of Christ is already united in one Spirit, whether we act like it or not. We are called to maintain that unity—the fellowship of believers, the relationships we have with God and with each other. We do that by treating one another the way God treats each of us. In Jesus, He demonstrated humility, gentleness, patience, and bearing with one another. He puts up with our idiosyncrasies, endures long seasons of our ignorance or disobedience, reaches us with His kindness and gentleness, and then tells us to exhibit exactly the same character. We freely give what we have received from him (Matt. 10:8)—and make every effort to do that in a way that preserves the unity of believers.

Why Transformation Is Bigger Than We Think

God is extremely interested in your transformation for your sake. It is the only way for you to experience a meaningful, fulfilling life according to your design. Your spiritual renaissance is taking you all the way back to your original, God-given purpose and all the way forward into an eternity with Him. So, in a sense, this transformation is about you.

But it's not *just* about you. In fact, it's unfathomably bigger than each of us. Paul has made that clear in the majestic, expansive words and pictures he has given us in the first three chapters of this letter, and he points to the big picture again here. "There is one body and one Spirit, just as you were called to one hope when you were called; one Lord, one faith, one baptism; one God and Father of all, who is over all and through all and in all" (Eph. 4:4–6). We are part of something infinitely bigger than our own lives.

The statements in these three verses seem to crescendo into an overarching truth: that the body of Christ, the church, must reflect His character. We have both an individual calling and a corporate calling to be Christlike. That's why our transformation happens in the context of relationships. We can't be the body of Christ as separate, independent individuals. We may look around at the church today, wonder why it is so fragmented, and think the prayers of Jesus for unity were unanswered (John 17:11, 20–23). But whether we act united or not, we are in fact part of one body. We *are* united. Paul calls us here to live like it.

Some of the most moving experiences in my Christian life have been witnessing unity in the body of Christ. I will never forget teaching in the Middle East to a mixed group of leaders and pastors from all across the region. As I taught about spiritual warfare and the strongholds of resentment and unforgiveness, a believer from Iraq stood up and confessed his sin and apologized to a fellow believer from Iran. They had both been soldiers in the Iran–Iraq War. In the midst of 150 fellow leaders, these two men stood, forgave each other for past hatred and atrocities, and cried and embraced. They demonstrated what unity among believers looks like.

The original text does not begin with "there is." Without any bridge between the preceding phrase about keeping the unity of the Spirit through the bond of peace, the next three verses continue with "one body and one Spirit." The wording makes an emphatic connection between the Spirit's peaceful, unifying effect and the underlying foundation of our unity.

That foundation is one body, one Spirit, one hope, one Lord, one faith, one baptism, and one God and Father over, through, and in all (vv. 5–6). This staccato progression includes each member of the Trinity, emphasizes the word "one" seven times, emphasizes the word "all" four times, and brings together everyone who is in Christ under the sovereignty of God.

There are two triads of "ones." The first is one body, one Spirit, and one hope. The body is us, the church. The Holy Spirit brought the church into existence and draws each of us into it through Christ. And as members of one body under one Spirit, we have a lot in common: a shared fellowship, a shared mission to the world, and a hope of heaven and our ultimate calling.

The second triad focuses on the Son. There is one Lord (Jesus), one faith (our belief in Him), and one baptism (signifying our entrance into His resurrected life). Our baptism suggests not just a water ceremony but our shared identity. We have all come into the church through Jesus as Lord. Our one faith is rooted in our one Lord as we are baptized into Him alone.

The list ends with a sovereign summary: "One God and Father of all, who is over all and through all and in all." This brief phrase manages to highlight both the divine nature and the personal character of God. He is God without equal or competitor, but He is also Father, drawing close to us in love. So the sequence that begins with the unity of God the Spirit leads through the lordship of Christ to the sovereignty of God the Father. He's over all, in all, through all. He's got your situation and everyone else's under control.

Think of what that means for your life. The overall impact of these verses elevates your calling beyond just you. Your renaissance is not just about God's plan for you. His specific purposes for you are important, and you have every reason to follow them with all your heart. But His overarching purposes for the church and the

You get to be part of that enormous, eternity-shaping plan. That ought to get you up in the morning. Your personal transformation takes on cosmic significance.

world are bigger. You get to be part of that enormous, eternity-shaping plan. That ought to get you up in the morning. Your personal transformation takes on cosmic significance.

When we begin to think that our transformation is only about us—our personal happiness, fulfillment, and growth—we lose sight of the big picture. Jesus did have a lot to say about His desires for us individually and the joy He wants us to have. He wants our joy to be full and our lives to be abundant. But that all fits within a vast and staggering vision for the fullness of God's kingdom. Our transformation is imperative because our lives are mini-expressions of the reality of Jesus. Paul draws our attention to the theological galaxy of His goodness to remind us that our individual lives joined together in the church, the body of Christ, form a larger expression of God's immeasurable love for the world.

All of Ephesians has been leading up to these verses. After telling us who we are in Christ, commanding believers to live as transformed people according to our new identity, identifying the relationships and attitudes that make this transformation possible, Paul now explains the enormity of what is at stake. The universe's attention is not centered on your devotional life or mine. Our personal fulfillment and purposes are not the highest stakes. What is at stake is the reality of the Godhead's unity expressed in and through this miraculous creation He calls the church.

Do you remember when we talked about spiritual myopia? This is the antidote. When our lives don't reflect what we believe, we are missing out on the bigger picture. We are like walking billboards that proclaim, "*Not* one body, *not* one Spirit, *not* one hope, *not* one

Lord, *not* one faith, *not* one baptism, *not* one God and Father over, through, and in all." We buy into the world's philosophy of "to each his own"—or, in more current language, "whatever." If all those "ones" are real, our lives need to reflect reality. Our spiritual myopia needs corrective lenses.

Good corrective lenses will give us a high view of God. We need to come back to biblical Christianity, to rediscover our roots, to experience a cultural renaissance in the church that opens up the majesty of God's plan before us like a new world. That will mean sometimes shutting off the TV or closing down the phone or laptop to read, think, pray, and discuss what we're learning about God and how He's working in our lives. Like the scholars, philosophers, and artists of the Renaissance, go back to those fundamental questions about why we're here, what really matters, and what our destiny is. Memorize great passages of Scripture and meditate on them throughout the day. Read great books about God and thought-provoking devotionals and talk about them. Let the sounds of great worship music fill your ears, your heart, and even your mouth whenever you can. (I've listed some resources at the end of this chapter that have helped me do this.) Far too many Christians have let shallow teaching and superficial experiences dumb down the gospel, and as a result, they now avoid the kinds of questions that stretch us and create the capacity within our souls to grow and be transformed. We need to be expanded. We need a renewed, revived, reborn view of God. We need a spiritual renaissance!

Have fun with that—literally. You may find a new motivation and zeal springing up in your heart. You'll probably discover that your prayers are deepening and your joy is growing fuller. You'll definitely find it harder to blend in with the culture and become like the many Christians who have given up on the idea of real change. Your life will become richer and fuller—or, as Jesus put it, more abundant—by your increasing awareness that God is both intensely interested in every detail of your life and delighted to make you a vital piece to the massive, cosmic reflection of who He is. You will experience the wonder and awe of His nature.

As wonderful as it is to fulfill your design as the image of God by conforming to Christ, you are not enough to provide the full picture. He is an infinite God with a multitude of facets that we have only begun to realize. That's why His plan draws multitudes of people from diverse places, backgrounds, cultures, and perspectives into His body—a vast, unified mosaic that better reflects His image than one human being can do. It's a breathtaking privilege to be a part of that. And it's yours.

Envision This Glorious Renaissance

As much as you may want to change, as much as you recognize that genuine happiness and blessedness occurs only as you are being conformed to the image of Christ, and as wonderful as the benefits of your transformation are to the people around you, your motivations for change go much deeper than personal experiences and rewards. Your transformation becomes part of a larger transformation, a kingdom renaissance that reconnects a broken world with its original design and builds on an eternal foundation. As Paul pointed out earlier in this letter, we are chosen before the foundation of the world, collectively and individually, to "the praise of his glory" (Eph. 1:12, 14) and "to bring unity to all things in heaven and on earth under Christ" (1:10). We are seated with Him above all things (1:20–22; 2:6), He does immeasurable things through the power that works within us (3:20), and as a body of believers, we have become "the fullness of him who fills everything in every way" (1:23). We have entered into a glory we can hardly imagine.

If you look in the mirror and realize your life has not changed significantly enough since you came to Christ, please do not despair. Lift up your eyes and look beyond yourself. You are not the source of your own transformation; Jesus is. Catch a vision for who He is, what He has done for you, how He is working in this world and through His people, and how you can become part of the glorious picture that reflects His glory. He is never looking to condemn you or focus on your imperfections but to call forward the Christ within you. That's your focus too. It isn't an easy or speedy transformation, but it is guaranteed to those who persevere in faith, embracing the humility, gentleness, and patience of His nature. And in your relationships with the body of Christ— and even the world beyond—you will see the Spirit of God rising up within you, empowering you, and reshaping your attitudes, desires, and experiences.

> *Lift up your eyes and look beyond yourself. You are not the source of your own transformation; Jesus is.*

Capture the wonder of this renaissance. Your new life is full of adventure. No good adventure will lead you down easy and comfortable paths, but those in the kingdom of God will always lead you onward and upward into joyful fulfillment. You are anchored in a certain foundation, empowered by God's own Spirit, and being restored into the image of the One who called you and made you His own. Your rebirth into the kingdom of God does not leave you at its doorstep. This renaissance draws you ever closer into the arms of the Father who is over all, through all, and in all.

Helpful Resources for Expanding Your View of God

These resources are only a small sampling of what is available, but these have been particularly helpful to me in developing a high view of God and helping me see the big picture of His purposes. It also helps to memorize classic passages like Isaiah 40, Psalm 145, Romans 12, or Matthew 5–7; listen to worship music that focuses on God's glory, majesty, goodness, and love; and speak His promises and purposes out loud so your heart and mind get used to hearing them as truth.

A. W. Tozer. *The Knowledge of the Holy: The Attributes of God, Their Meaning in the Christian Life.* San Francisco: Harper & Row, 1961.

J. I. Packer. *Knowing God.* Downers Grove, IL: InterVarsity, 1973.

J. P. Moreland. *Love God with All Your Mind: The Role of Reason in the Life of the Soul.* 1997; repr., Colorado Springs: NavPress, 2012.

Dallas Willard. *The Spirit of the Disciplines: Understanding How God Changes Lives.* San Francisco: Harper & Row, 1988.

Dallas Willard. *Life without Lack: Living in the Fullness of Psalm 23.* Nashville: Thomas Nelson, 2018.

Francis Schaeffer. *True Spirituality: How to Live for Jesus Moment by Moment.* Carol Stream, IL: Tyndale House Publishers, 1971.

Dr. and Mrs. Howard Taylor. *Hudson Taylor's Spiritual Secret.* 1932; repr., Chicago: Moody Publishers, 2009.

CHAPTER 4

Where Do We Get the Power to Change?

EPHESIANS 4:7-10

Hudson Taylor was a missionary to China in the 1800s and, by almost all accounts, an unusually fruitful and effective servant of God. He was known for an unwavering commitment to his calling, making great sacrifices, and tirelessly working to bring people into a saving relationship with Jesus. But at a point of exhaustion many years into his ministry, he realized something so significant and profound that it transformed his entire approach to the Christian life. This dedicated Christian who had already earned a reputation for fruitful service to God discovered a new perspective that changed everything—so much so that he said he had become "a new man."

Hudson Taylor's story greatly impacted my own life. His "spiritual secret" is a profound insight about how we access the power of the Holy Spirit in our lives. It's what he and others have called "the exchanged life." He realized that our old nature died with Jesus on the cross, and we now receive His life in exchange. Instead of striving for faith and holiness, we consider our old selves to be dead and instead rest in the strength of the One who is faithful and holy.

Most new Christians strive and strain to experience their new life, and over time, they get really tired. Maybe you can relate to that. The constant effort to become someone new is exhausting. But the solution is not what most would expect. It's completely counter-intuitive. In the kingdom of God, we get strength through weakness, greatness through servanthood, abundance through giving, and life through death. These are paradoxes that even Jesus' closest followers struggled with. But they are fundamental to the change we long for.

We even see this principle at work in nature. An acorn has all the makings of an oak tree in it. The oak's DNA, the programming for its entire future, is already there. It doesn't look like a tree, and it won't for a long time. But when it is fully grown, it will be one of the strongest, sturdiest plants on earth. It will grow beautiful leaves, provide plenty of shade, color autumn with magnificent artistry, and shape vast landscapes with its imposing presence. It will be glorious.

But something must happen to that acorn for it to become a mighty oak tree. It has to fall to the ground, be covered with soil, and lose all appearances of ever having been a seed. It essentially dies as a seed in order to be reborn as an oak. The sprout, then seedling, then sapling will endure harsh seasons, strong winds, bright sun, and maybe even floods and droughts. All those trials just make it a hardier plant. It will eventually grow to maturity and be admired by many. But that end result cannot happen without that first descent into the ground.

Jesus referred to that planting process the night before His crucifixion. He knew He would have to fall to the ground and die in order to live and produce many more seeds (John 12:24). But then He immediately shifted the focus from Himself to His followers. Not only must He enter into the ground and die in order to come up again as a life-giving, fruit-bearing plant; so must they. "Anyone who loves their life will lose it, while anyone who hates their life in this world will keep it for eternal life" (v. 25). Paul referred to the same principle of seeds being sown into death and then growing into life. We sow what is perishable, dishonorable, weak, and natural in order to be raised as imperishable, honorable, powerful, and supernatural (1 Cor. 15:36–37, 42–44). In other words, we can't become who we were meant to be without giving up who we were. The seed has to die in order to live.

That's a foundational principle not only in entering into eternal life but in living it out. Like a seed planted in the ground, we are called to walk through a process of participating in the death of Jesus, of being planted in the tomb, so we can rise out of it in new life. It isn't a onetime experience; it's an ongoing dynamic. As far as God is concerned, old things have already passed away and new things have come (2 Cor. 5:17). From our position at ground level, however, we still experience remnants of old things, and they have to undergo a death. We have to learn to apply His death and resurrection in order to live resurrected lives.

> *Like a seed planted in the ground, we are called to walk through a process of participating in the death of Jesus, of being planted in the tomb, so we can rise out of it in new life.*

Transformation really only happens when we approach it as an all-or-nothing proposition, which can feel really intimidating and overwhelming. Acorns don't try on some sprouts and leaves before deciding to go all in. They can't start and then take it back, then grow a few inches higher and shrink a few inches lower while they're figuring it all out. Their investment in oakhood is a total commitment.

I've known many people who talk a lot about change but can't quite pull the trigger to make it happen—alcoholics who swear they are going to quit drinking right after the next drink, or would-be exercisers promising to start back at the gym next week, next month, or next year, only to never quite get there. I've known Christians who agonize over their lack of change while never actually doing the things that bring about change. But an acorn's intentions aren't enough. It actually has to fall to the ground.

In contrast to people whose change never comes, I've seen many people who were so bound in sinful behaviors that escape looked humanly impossible, and still they were freed to grow and thrive. I've seen people who appeared to lack character become surprisingly fruitful in the body of Christ. Their transformation has been startling, and it has happened not because they embarked on a plan for improvement but because they knew how to die to the old and live in the new.

> **I've known Christians who agonize over their lack of change while never actually doing the things that bring about change.**

The greatest obstacle to our transformation is our sin. That sounds like a harsh assessment, but that's what it is. When we're selfish, envious, lustful, demanding, and hurtful, we're interfering with our own path to maturity. When we do the right things for the wrong reasons—to impress, to seek attention, to people-please, to gain some ego-building reward—that's sin too. In every case, our flesh (the old) is in control, and the Holy Spirit (the new) isn't. So if sin is our biggest obstacle to real, lasting change, it has to be dealt with.

The problem is that we don't have the resources in our own nature to deal with it. We can't overcome the flesh in the power of the flesh. It has long been under control of the power of sin. God's solution to sin was not just to forgive it but to strip it of power by putting it to death. He did that by sending Jesus to the cross.

The next section of Ephesians 4 explains how Jesus' death and resurrection apply to our death to the old nature and renaissance into the new, which enables us to live in our new identity in Him. Paul's teaching here parallels another passage, where he makes it clear that continuing to live in sin is not an option for a Christian because we have died to it (Rom. 6:1–4). We have been baptized into Jesus' death and buried with Him in order to be raised with Him into new life (vv. 3–4). We can't live the resurrected life until we understand that we have died—and count on that death being true (v. 11). Death is a prerequisite for resurrection. It's not the end; it's the beginning.

What Was Jesus Doing?

Understanding what it means to identify with Jesus' death is so critical for our transformation process that Paul explained exactly what Jesus was doing between the time He died on the cross and was resurrected from the grave. He uses some ancient warfare language no longer familiar to us to describe Jesus' victory over death, sin, and the devil. The historical background is fascinating, but the main point is clear. Understanding Jesus' mission between the time He died on the cross and His resurrection helps us grasp with our hearts, minds, and souls how His death applies to our new life in Him.

When we understand that, we can appropriate the grace already available to us to face the same opponents Jesus faced: death, sin, and Satan. We begin to see sin and temptation not as unbeatable foes but as humiliated, defeated enemies. By grace through faith, we can overcome their power and walk in freedom. We can experience the resurrected life He promised.

Paul's words in this passage are obscure to most modern minds, yet they are powerful in their implications.

But to each one of us grace has been given as Christ apportioned it. This is why it says: "When he ascended on high, he took many captives and gave gifts to his people." (What does "he ascended" mean except that he also descended to the lower, earthly regions? He who descended is the very one who ascended higher than all the heavens, in order to fill the whole universe.) (Eph. 4:7–10)

The first few words base the rest of the passage on the generosity of Christ's grace. Paul introduces a quote from Psalm 68:18 about God ascending, taking captives, and giving gifts and applies these words to Jesus, specifically to the events between His crucifixion and resurrection.

If Jesus ascended, Paul argues, then He must have also descended into the lower parts of the earth. This seems to be a reference to Hades or Sheol, Greek and Hebrew terms for the place of the dead. And if He ascended, He did so in order "to fill the whole universe." Without any background, those are mystifying words. But a dramatic picture emerges when we unpack the historical and cultural context, and it gives us a whole new perspective on what Jesus actually accomplished for us. So let's break this down by its key phrases.

He took many captives. About fifty years before Jesus, Julius Caesar spent years in Gaul trying to bring it under complete Roman control. Many of the locals resisted, and Caesar ruthlessly put down many rebellions. The climactic battle involved an attack against Roman forces by massive numbers of Gauls led by their chieftain, Vercingetorix. The Gauls almost broke through Roman lines, but Caesar prevailed. Vercingetorix is said to have surrendered the next day by dismounting his horse in front of Caesar, stripping himself of armor, laying down his weapons, and submitting to captivity along with many of his men. The defeated chieftain was taken to

Rome and later, with Caesar's chariot leading the way in a spectac-
ular triumph, paraded in humiliating fashion to symbolize Rome's
invincibility before being killed.

This stripping and humiliation of enemies was a common practice in ancient warfare, and winning commanders usually distributed the spoils of war to their armies. Every Jew who had lived in
the previous centuries and every Greek or Roman reading Paul's
words would have understood the picture he presents in this passage. Long city sieges often ended with such a spectacle of victory
(see 2 Sam. 12:26–31 and 2 Kings 25 for biblical examples). Roman
triumphs (victory parades) were well-known spectacles featuring
the conquering general and his troops in shining armor dragging
defeated foes behind. This is Paul's picture of Jesus. Our conquering King not only defeated the enemy. He stripped him of power,
humiliated him in triumph, led captives away, and gave His people
all the enemy's possessions—in this case, spiritual power.

Paul's purpose in this portrayal is to help us understand the reason for our spiritual gifts. Jesus won the battle over sin, death, and
the devil and gives the same victory to His followers. Between the
cross and the resurrection, Jesus defeated Satan's kingdom and is
turning it over to His people.

He descended to the lower, earthly regions. The grammar here
is ambiguous, referring either to the lower parts (which are) the earth
or the lower parts (of) the earth. But the latter seems to better fit
Paul's purpose here. In Jewish belief, the place of the dead was *Sheol*
(Greek *Hades*), which contained a compartment for the wicked dead
and another for the righteous. We see this division in Jesus' parable in
Luke 16:19–31, in which a self-centered rich man went to the abode
of the wicked and Lazarus went to paradise, or "Abraham's bosom."
A great chasm separated the two, but they could see each other.

Jesus entered into this abode of the dead between His crucifixion and resurrection. According to Peter, He first went to the
punishment side to preach to the spirits in prison (1 Peter 3:19).
He was not inviting demonic forces to repent and be saved. He was
declaring the victory of the cross: *The work of salvation is finished.
Sin's power has been broken. The sting of death is gone. You are a defeated foe.*

Jesus also visited the paradise section of the afterlife and
preached to those who are now dead—Old Testament believers—
so they could live in the spirit (1 Peter 4:6). This word for "preach"
is different from the one Peter used for Jesus' words in the abode of
the wicked. It's the good news. Jesus visited paradise to inform and
confirm the faith of Old Testament saints.

Every believer from every time period is saved on the same basis:
the work of Christ on the cross as the substitutionary payment for
sin. Old Testament believers looked forward to it; we look back to
it. Everyone can look to Jesus and see that God has done what He
promised to do.

In order to fill the whole universe. Jesus came to demonstrate what has always been true—that He is Lord. He visited the
most God-forsaken place in creation to claim His sovereignty as
ruler and deliverer of the universe over all that can and cannot be
seen. The song of the redeemed in Revelation captures this fullness
beautifully:

> They sang a new song, saying: "You are worthy to take the scroll and
> to open its seals, because you were slain, and with your blood you
> purchased for God persons from every tribe and language and peo-
> ple and nation. You have made them to be a kingdom and priests to
> serve our God, and they will reign on the earth."
> Then I looked and heard the voice of many angels, numbering

thousands upon thousands, and ten thousand times ten thousand. They encircled the throne and the living creatures and the elders. In a loud voice they were saying: "Worthy is the Lamb, who was slain, to receive power and wealth and wisdom and strength and honor and glory and praise!"

Then I heard every creature in heaven and on earth and under the earth and on the sea, and all that is in them, saying: "To him who sits on the throne and to the Lamb be praise and honor and glory and power, for ever and ever!" (Rev. 5:9–13)

That takes us back to our original question in this section. What was Jesus doing between the time of His death on the cross and the moment of His resurrection? He was establishing His right to reclaim all of creation. He was declaring that He had defeated sin, death, and Satan. In space-time, objective history, He was providing the basis for your spiritual freedom and transformation.

The Power to Change

Your transformation is possible not because you are empowered to do better but because you have died with Jesus. Not only was the penalty of your sin broken once and for all. So was the power of your sin and its control over your life. The enemy is now a defeated foe, subject to the authority of the Spirit of Christ and the Word of God dwelling within you. These are crucial, bedrock truths of your new life in Him.

Please understand that this is not just a theological concept or a legal transaction that you will be able to appreciate in heaven one day. It is here-and-now reality. You are organically connected to Jesus in such a way that when you accepted Him as your Savior,

The enemy is now a defeated foe, subject to the authority of the Spirit of Christ and the Word of God dwelling within you.

you died with Him and were resurrected with Him. Like the seed, your old nature has been planted in the ground and your new nature rises up above it. All of the benefits of Jesus' victory over sin, death, and Satan are yours.

This is why Paul so emphatically told his readers to "reckon" (NKJV) or "consider" (NASB) themselves dead to sin but alive to God in Christ (Rom. 6:11). The vast majority of Christians are striving for death to sin and life in Christ, *but we already have them!* This is our reality, and it becomes our experience as we count on it by faith to be so.

Perhaps you don't feel as if the siege of sin in your life has been broken. Maybe the archenemy still seems very alive. Unfortunately, this amazing work of Christ and the journey between the cross and the resurrection—a vivid, captivating, powerful image to Paul's first readers—has been reduced to what we normally call the Easter story. The message has been boiled down to the minimum of Jesus coming, dying for our sin, rising from the dead, and offering us forgiveness if we accept Him as our Savior—all wonderfully true, and a powerful message, but not the whole story. The gospel goes much deeper. Profound events happened that turn dying seeds into immense forests of mighty oaks. Jesus made genuine transformation possible.

> **Sadly, most Christians don't change very much because they really have no clue what they already possess or what happened to them when they trusted Christ as their Savior.**

Sadly, most Christians don't change very much because they really have no clue what they already possess or what happened to them when they trusted Christ as their Savior. We need to understand that the same power that raised Jesus from the dead is at work within us right now (Rom. 8:11; Eph. 1:19; 3:20).

But remember, the power of resurrection implies a death. You can't be raised up if you haven't gone down. Only as we believe old things to be dead can we experience the newness of life. So let's get practical and talk about how this actually works in our everyday lives.

In our focus passage for this chapter, Ephesians 4:7–10, Paul explained three profound theological truths that help us understand the basis for personal transformation.

1. Life-Change Always Begins with the Truth

Life-change doesn't begin with an experience. It may involve an experience, and experiences can open our eyes to needs and possibilities, but transformation is rooted in objective truth. The night before His crucifixion, Jesus prayed that the Father would make His followers pure and holy by the truth—God's Word (John 17:17). Scripture is at the root of our transformation into Jesus' likeness.

Jesus told His followers, "If you abide in My word [which means to take it in and act on it], you are My disciples indeed. And you shall know the truth, and the truth shall make you free" (John 8:31–32 NKJV). In other words, if we cling to the spiritual DNA God has put within us—that Jesus is the living Word, and His Spirit dwells in our hearts—we can become free of the same old habits we used to struggle with, the same attitudes, lusts, and misplaced values that used to weigh us down, and live and love authentically. This kind of change is possible. Jesus prayed it and gave His word to His followers.

Ephesians 4 is one of those places in God's Word where liberating truth is spelled out for us. Because of the victory Jesus won at the cross and in His resurrection, because He has given us the spoils of victory, we have the power to live a new life. Anyone can try to do good, adopt a new code of ethics, and become more moral. That's great, but that doesn't reflect the depth of victory Jesus has given us. It's a relationship, and in that fellowship between us and God's Spirit within us, He is working to give us the desire and power to do what pleases Him (Phil. 2:13). It's a relationship grounded in truth.

This truth touches every area of our lives. We don't have to sin, be addicted to any substances or behaviors, live in fear of death or anything else, be anxious about the future, be victimized by circumstances or anyone's decisions (including our own), or feel defeated by dysfunctional relationships or oppressive problems. Sin, death, and the adversary of our souls are defeated foes. Do we still experience the ravages of sin all around us? Sure. Does it have any control over us? Absolutely not. The only power sin, death, and Satan now have is the power we give them.

We don't have to be deceived by the world's system or its values anymore. We don't have to be sucked into the ads and cravings of a self-centered culture. We have no reason to become depressed when the world's promises and strategies fail. Jesus disarmed, displayed, and destroyed the works of the great deceiver (Col. 2:13–15). He who is in us is greater than he who is in the world (1 John 4:4). The blinders are off, the light has come on, the deception is exposed. That means we are not bound by any false promises, values, or systems. We are free to change. And genuine change always begins with the truth.

2. Life-Change Demands That We Act on the Truth

Knowing the truth isn't enough. It's a start, but a lot of people know things they don't act on, and their knowledge has no practical effect in their lives. We implement knowledge first by faith, then by actually taking steps backed by our faith. We act on the truth.

Notice what Paul's picture of Christ between cross and resurrection implies. We become partakers of His victory over sin, death, and Satan. We join the winning side the moment we receive Him as our Savior. This is a true, objective, historical reality that remains practically irrelevant to us until we ask Jesus by faith to come into our lives, not only to save us but to live in us daily. The Spirit of God comes in, our sins are forgiven, and we spend the rest of eternity "in Christ." As spiritual babies, we begin the process of transformation, putting away the old and embracing the new, cooperating with God to conform us to the likeness of His Son

This again goes back to how we see ourselves. If we claim that the Spirit of Jesus is living through us and empowering us but still see ourselves as sinners who are inevitably going to fail, there's a contradiction between the truth and our faith. We are putting more stock in our experiences of failure than in His victory over sin, death, and the enemy. If we see ourselves as participants in the divine nature (2 Peter 1:4), we can trample on sin, stare death in the face, and live as people who are absolutely convinced that nothing can separate us from the love of God. He is working all things together for our good, and we are more than conquerors in Him (Rom. 8:28, 37–39). We can actually know—and very often sense—the power of the Holy Spirit rising up within us to overcome.

That's why the question about Christian growth and transformation is never fundamentally about whether you go to church, live morally, give to good causes, try hard, and send up a prayer from time to time. Religion is a matter

Have you acted on the truth God has given you?

of good, honest efforts to do better. The relationship we have entered into by faith is a matter of a supernatural source empowering us from within based on the authority of God's unfailing Word. It embeds the divine DNA within us. It takes our old nature into the grave and exchanges it for an entirely new nature from the moment we believe. It gives us a vision of eternal realities, including the truth about who God is and who we are in Him. Since human beings live according to the vision we have, we can stop falling prey to the same deceptions that once blinded us because our new eyes see everything in a new light.

Have you acted on the truth God has given you? If you have asked Him to be your Savior and Lord, do you see yourself as having died and risen with Him? Are you taking steps daily to live out your new identity, embrace the divine nature implanted within you, and exercise your victory over sin, death, and the enemy? Have you left the acorn behind so you can grow into a strong, fruit-bearing tree?

3. Life-Change Is Both a Gift and a Responsibility

Only God can transform us. But as we've seen, that doesn't mean we sit passively by while He works on us. We can't change on our own, but He chooses not to change us unilaterally without our cooperation. As new creations, we enjoy specific privileges and carry out specific responsibilities in the life-change process.

Human beings can plant seeds, but we can't make them grow. Farmers and arborists know this; they choose the right environment, till or prepare the ground, plant, water, fertilize, and protect. But they can't cause growth. The transformation from seed to mature plants and harvests is a partnership between human practices and God's provision.

Paul used this illustration when he wrote to the Corinthian church about their transformation. "I planted the seed in your hearts, and Apollos watered it, but it was God who made it grow. It's not important who does the planting, or who does the watering. What's important is that God makes the seed grow" (1 Cor. 3:6–7 NLT). It's really important in our process of change to see God as the one who empowers and provides. But it's just as important to actually create the right environment for ourselves and cultivate what

God has entrusted to us. Many Christians think transformation is just a matter of developing the right disciplines through willpower and persistence. But discipline is a tool of cultivation, not the empowerment itself. Growth from the inside out requires our participation in and appropriation of God's power. We will discuss the role of prayer, God's Word, and God's people as conduits of grace and power in later chapters.

If we were only looking for outward transformation, that distinction between self-discipline and God's power might not matter very much. Most people can change their outward behavior with the right motivation and environment. But God's transforming work goes deeper into our secret thoughts, our capacity to love, and our innermost desires. He frees us from long-standing addictions, calms tormented minds, and enables us to be the spouse or parent or friend we've always wanted to be.

When you are confident that God really loves you and empowers you, you can take steps of faith and trust Him to respond. He will flood you with grace to become the husband or wife your mate has longed for but never seen, the mom or dad your kids crave, the selfless, undemanding person who loves unconditionally rather than waiting for the other person to show love. By the grace of God, you can go ahead and give the love that the people around you need rather than waiting for responses you might think you deserve. Only God can work those miracles. He produces supernatural changes within.

The Gift of Grace

It's easy to get caught up in the fascinating background of Ephesians 4:7–10 and forget the primary purpose of the passage, which will lead into the next section of the letter. Paul's point about Jesus' victory is that God has supernaturally endowed every believer with gifts of grace (v. 7). These gifts are empowered by His Spirit to help other believers in the process of transformation. The moment we receive Christ, we also receive a supernatural ability that allows us to share the grace of God with others. We participate with God in our own transformation, but we also participate with Him and others in their transformation. We give and receive grace through the gifts God has given to each of us.

The term used for God's gift of grace in verse 7 is not the same as the one used elsewhere for spiritual gifts, which have to do with our specific area of service. This gift is about our capacity for service. It's a sacred trust. Everyone has it "as Christ apportioned it," measured to fit who we are so our life and purpose will achieve God's highest glory and bring about the greatest joy in our lives. In other words, God's grace and gifts are tailor-made for each of us.

Grace is God's unmerited favor. That means there is nothing we can do to deserve it or earn it. He gives grace not only through His Spirit and His Word but also through the lives of other people. That's why our transformation is not only a gift but also a responsibility. Only God can bring about change, but He never chooses to do it alone. He works through Christians loving one another in community and operating in each of our areas of giftedness in a way that allows transformation to occur. When we live in authentic community, we act as catalysts for change in each other's lives.

He gives grace not only through His Spirit and His Word but also through the lives of other people. That's why our transformation is not only a gift but also a responsibility.

I can think of at least two reasons for this relational dynamic. One is that living in community with other believers reminds us that life-change comes through grace, not self-effort. We are not on our own. The church is like the soil and climate in which saplings grow into strong oaks. Spiritual gifts of grace mutually applied remind us constantly that our process is not about trying hard and earning God's favor. It's about grace.

The other reason for community is to empower us as others-centered agents of grace who supply what others need to become Christlike. God uses each believer's spiritual gifts as tools and resources as we live in humility, love, and genuine relationship together. We are transformed by the gifts others bring into the fellowship, and we are also transformed in using our gifts to minister to others. God uses the truth of His Word, the faith of believers, and the grace apportioned to each of His people to bring about supernatural transformation.

Perhaps that's one of the reasons so many people are not experiencing the change they long for. They are going about it on their own. Even if they see their new selves accurately and are grounding themselves in God's Word, they are not benefiting from the grace given to them through others. God has arranged His body so that no one person has every spiritual gift, which means that you can't experience everything you need from God on your own. Other members of the body have what you need, and you each have what other members of the body need. Grace is multifaceted, and no one person can receive its many facets in isolation from the diverse believers who are called to reflect Him. When you understand that your gifts and the gifts of others are designed to work together and connect in authentic community with the fellowship of believers, God uses that environment to carry out His transforming work.

A Personal Example of Life-Change

I got a clear picture of this transformation process pretty early in my Christian experience. My dad was brought up in a strong, moral, "culturally Christian" home, but he was not a Christian. He grew up during the Depression, his father died when he was thirteen, and either by his mother's permission or by lying about his age, he went off to fight in the south Pacific when he was under eighteen. I knew he lived with the nightmares of killing hundreds in Guam and Iwo Jima and feeling deeply guilty about surviving the war, but like a lot of ex-Marines, he stuffed his feelings and coped with the help of three packs a day and plenty of alcohol. But he was a committed father, and I learned to appreciate what he had overcome in life.

Over the years, Dad drank more and more to escape and became increasingly absent. By the time I hit high school, my mom gave him an ultimatum—his alcohol or his family. Dad chose well; he went even further than her ultimatum and quit drinking *and* smoking. But he still didn't understand his guilt or deal with his issues. He didn't realize he couldn't solve his problems on his own.

I eventually left for college, and one by one, my family members became Christians. I had seen how different my sister's life was after accepting Christ, and thanks to her influence and the Fellowship of Christian Athletes, I was introduced to Jesus. The bricklayer who discipled me had been trained by The Navigators. I began to read the Bible voraciously, and God began to change my desires. Nobody told me what I needed to do or not do to be a good Christian. I just read the Bible morning and evening and was around a group of loving, authentic people who were living out the gospel. I saw God change them and experienced Him changing me.

I returned home after my freshman year to find that God was working in the rest of my family. Dad was restless, and one day he asked, "Chip, what has happened to you? You're different. You have a peace in your life I've never seen before."

"Well, Dad, I asked Christ to come into my life about a year ago."

I had been reluctant to tell my parents because it was all so new to me. So I was astonished when Dad said, "Son, whatever you have, I think I need it."

I had never tried to put my faith into words for someone else. I managed to say, "Dad, all I know is that I started reading the Bible, and I prayed a prayer, and then a lot of things started changing inside me."

So that's where Dad started. As a good Marine, he did it the right way—up at 5:30 every morning to read the Bible for an hour. For three months, he read the four gospels. It took him a while to realize these were four overlapping biographies of Jesus. But he kept at it. He didn't know it, but a big change was coming because life-change always begins with the truth. It isn't just an experience, an activity, an event, church attendance, being a good person, or occasionally praying. It's rooted in truth.

After about three months of reading the Gospels, Dad said he still felt like he was on the outside looking in. "How do I get in?" he asked.

"I don't know, Dad. Just keep reading." I could see the spiritual hunger in his eyes.

There was so much he couldn't put into words, so he just nodded and said, "Okay."

After about three more months, he expanded into the rest of the New Testament. One day he said, "I still don't know what it's all about, but somewhere at the heart of this whole deal is faith. It just keeps coming up." He had hit upon the central theme of the New Testament. His discovery would transform him from a religious, churchgoing unbeliever to a child of God.

I know a lot of people who have been Christians for years who still don't understand that. They are still trying to clean up the outside with "oughts" and "shoulds" without their inner lives matching their claims. The seed of faith is just sitting there unplanted, uncultivated, untapped for its potential. They are still living lives of duty rather than delight.

God's greatest desire for us is that we would believe in the One who was sent (John 6:29; 17:20–23). That's what Dad discovered in the Gospels, and that became the turning point in his life because he acted on it. He later told me that during this time of searching, he walked by his dresser and saw a "Four Spiritual Laws" tract on it. He sat down and read through it, and the lights came on. He realized what it meant to have faith and place his trust in Christ's work on the cross and His resurrection. So with no fanfare, he closed his bedroom door, got down on his knees, and prayed the prayer printed in the back of that booklet. He admitted his sinfulness and realized that even the horrors he had been through during the war could be forgiven because of Christ's work on the cross. After six months of searching, he asked Jesus into his life. He acted on the truth he had received.

All of the principles we have discussed in this chapter were at work in my father's life. His transformation began with the truth, he acted on the truth, and he discovered that grace was both a gift and a responsibility as other Christians, particularly in our own family, demonstrated God's grace to him. My dad's life changed dramatically. He took the Bible seriously and within months found a solid Bible-teaching church and plugged in. Before long, my mom and dad were hosting a small group in their home, writing checks to fulfill the Great Commission, taking a course to learn to share their faith, and counseling people who, like themselves, were religious but didn't have a personal relationship with Christ.

Let Your Roots Grow Deep

A lot is packed into Ephesians 4:7–10, the four verses we've covered in this chapter. They present the basis of our transformation in the

cross and resurrection of Jesus, the resounding victory He declared
and implemented in the dark, obscure time between those two
events, and the grace He has given for our transformation through
the gifts He has distributed in His victory. Just as the first six verses
ended with a majestic, cosmic panorama of the stakes of our transformation, this section ends with an astounding picture of our participation in Jesus' triumph over sin, death, and evil. We are left
with a remarkable picture of what it takes to be transformed into
the image of our conquering Savior and King.

Perhaps it's surprising that our transformation into a new kind
of life follows the same trajectory as the one our unconventional
conqueror took to win that decisive battle. Through death with
Him—and through death to our old nature and ways—we are buried in the ground. But like the seed that dies and then lives, we are
born into something new. We are raised up with Jesus to live in
fellowship with His body, the people who believe and follow Him.
Our roots grow deep into His Word as we immerse ourselves in it
and act on it in trust. We are meant to find nourishment in the soil
of His church, grow in the climate of love and grace, and give and
receive the gifts He has given as the spoils of His victory. Over time,
supernatural things happen. We can't make ourselves grow, but we
can position ourselves and participate
in our growth by letting Him live His
life through us. As we do, we transform
into His likeness—strong, sturdy over-
comers of the winds, floods, droughts,
and storms that have come against us.

If you have never experienced this
kind of change, do whatever is necessary right now to enter into the new
life He freely gives. If you have never

> *If you have trusted
> in Him and the work
> He accomplished on
> the cross and in His
> resurrection, count
> on that reality daily,
> hourly, even moment
> by moment.*

trusted Him to take your old nature into the grave and bring you out in resurrection, place your faith in Him now and ask Him to come into your life. If you have trusted in Him and the work He accomplished on the cross and in His resurrection, count on that reality daily, hourly, even moment by moment. Embrace "the exchanged life" that so radically transformed Hudson Taylor's experience. Consider yourself dead to sin but alive to God in Christ. Root yourself thoroughly in the Word He has given you, take steps of faith according to His Word, and connect with other believers who minister the grace you need and who need the grace that is in you. Trust Him to transform you, and don't give up.

If you do that, I can promise that you will not be disappointed. You will be changed. God loves to do amazing things with ordinary lives. You can hardly imagine what He will do with yours, but it will be glorious. He will bring you into full maturity to tower above the landscape that once seemed so intimidating, offering the beauty and fruitfulness of His work in you for many to enjoy. You will be like a tree planted by streams of water (Ps. 1:3), a vital part of His eternal plan to fill the universe with His glory, experiencing and offering life in His wisdom, power, and love.

CHAPTER 5

Why Is It Impossible to Grow Alone?

EPHESIANS 4:11–13

f you've spent any time watching home-improvement shows on TV, you've seen plenty of examples of transformation. Often a married couple or partners in real estate and renovation, both with enormous know-how and creativity, take an out-of-date, sometimes dilapidated house and turn it into an amazingly beautiful place to live. They usually don't gut the original framework of the house, but everything else gets a makeover. The home takes on a truer, more lasting identity, a new version of its old self. The before-and-after pictures are quite a contrast. The end result very often brings the homeowner to tears of joy and appreciation.

These renovators don't start a project without a plan and just see where the work leads them. They have specific drawings and blueprints before they ever start. Rarely do they fund the project themselves. Their supply comes from the homeowner or the people who will buy the house at the end of the show. Along the way, they tear out everything that's old and replace it with new fixtures, surfaces, utilities, appliances, landscaping, furnishings, and colors. They pull in various experts and specialists to help them as needed. They become hands-on general contractors who rely on a larger team to get the job done. And by the end, they have created together a masterpiece of function and design.

Your new life in Christ is a lot like a renovation project. It's supplied by an unlimited source, the "one God and Father of all, who is over all and through all and in all" (Eph. 4:6). There is a very clear design plan, a blueprint that looks just like Jesus. This plan does not do away with your frame or your individual personality, but it does give you a new identity and purpose. A team of specialists is involved; they use the spiritual gifts God has given to His people through Christ's victory. You tear out the old things that no longer fit the vision of who you are becoming, and you replace them with new, Christlike features. And the end result, the contrast between before and after, is enough to bring us to tears of joy and appreciation.

God's Gift of Specialists

Up to this point, we have explored the foundations of our new life in Christ and the process of transformation into His image. But, as we've seen, the specifics of God's design involve other members of the team, the church. As Paul turns from the gift of grace apportioned to each believer to the various roles we play in each other's lives, He gives us a picture of how the design team functions as a whole—individual parts under the guidance and control of Jesus the overseer.

So Christ himself gave the apostles, the prophets, the evangelists, the pastors and teachers, to equip his people for works of service, so that the body of Christ may be built up until we all reach unity in the faith and in the knowledge of the Son of God and become mature, attaining to the whole measure of the fullness of Christ. (Eph. 4:11–13)

God has given His people a team of leaders, each with specific gifts and functions. Why? So the body of Christ may be built up in unity in the faith and in knowledge of Jesus, coming into the measure of His fullness. That's a big vision, and it can't be fulfilled without supernatural help. So leadership in the body of Christ is supernaturally empowered to develop and apply their gifts for the good of the body. The goal is to equip all Christians to use our gifts so that every member grows to maturity.

Jesus is the blueprint for that maturity. The gifted leaders who equip the saints for the work of ministry are working toward a vivid, Christlike result. When we reach our full potential spiritually, we think like Jesus, act like Jesus, love like Jesus, respond to our enemies like Jesus, and walk in the wisdom, character, power, and love of Jesus. He does a supernatural work in our lives through the equipping ministry of the body as a whole.

If you read this passage carefully, you may notice an unconventional template for leadership. The world's way of leadership is to put leaders at the top of a hierarchy to manage everyone beneath them. Historically, the church has fallen in line with that arrangement, and many Christians think the purpose of leadership is to do the work of ministry. The picture Paul gives us here puts leaders in a servant role of equipping everyone else so that *every* believer can do the work of ministry. It's an inverted pyramid, with the five ministry gifts listed in these verses supporting the entire body.

So how does the process actually work? You know the victory Christ has won, the death and resurrection you have in Him, the new identity He has given you, the Word of truth He has provided, the faith in His Word that puts steps to your beliefs, the gift and responsibility of His grace, and the organism called the church through which you give and receive His grace. But in terms of actually putting your renovation into practice, what's next? How do you get transformed from the inside out under the craftsmanship of God's Spirit and His team of specialists?

The practical blueprint begins to open up in this section of Ephesians. Paul provides specific instructions that will help transform you into the likeness of Christ. They explain how God meant for His church to function so that every single Christian can tap into the grace that God is working in and through His people. At the heart of the life-change God has promised is the way you fulfill your role in the body of Christ. So let's go back and look at this passage a little closer.

1. Leaders Are Gifted to Equip God's People for Service

This passage begins with a statement that "Christ himself gave." Transformation begins and ends with grace. God provides significant leaders in different places to help mature His body, but the focus is never supposed to be on the leaders. It's always on the One who gives the leaders. God never wants us to place spiritual leaders in places that only He can occupy. Our focus is not on catalysts for transformation or on the transformation itself. It's on the author, the One who transforms. He's the head of this project.

That said, Paul lists several important positions or gifts that form the foundation of leadership for the church:

Apostles. This term as it is used in the New Testament originally referred to anyone with a divine commission. It literally means "one who is sent." It's used in several ways in the New Testament and specifically applied to the twelve apostles, who were Jesus' closest disciples (minus Judas plus his replacement in Acts 1). But other people are called "apostle" too, including Barnabas (Acts 14:14), Silas and Timothy (1 Thess. 1:1; 2:6), James the brother of Jesus (Gal. 1:19), possibly Apollos (1 Cor. 4:6, 9), possibly Andronicus and Junia (Rom. 16:7), and of course Paul, who considered himself an apostle, was widely accepted as an apostle, and is often given that title prominently in our references to him today. At times, it refers only to those who were eyewitnesses to the risen Christ; at others, it refers simply to those who seem to have received a divine commission. Many people today use it to refer to people in pioneering and church-planting ministries, though it is sometimes more broadly applied to leaders of equipping ministries.

Some uses of the New Testament word—for example, as a reference to eyewitnesses of Jesus' earthly ministry—have already been fulfilled. Their testimony is carried on throughout the ages in the Scriptures and the doctrinal foundations they left us. Modern uses of the term are interpreted in a variety of ways by different denominations and streams of thought. What should never be lost in that discussion, however, is Paul's purpose in mentioning them here. The apostolic gift was never given to establish a group of spiritual elites who do the primary work of ministry. It was given so these leaders could equip every believer to do the work of ministry.

Prophets. The second group on Paul's list is prophets. Most people think of biblical prophets as fire-breathing preachers like Elijah or predictors of the future like Isaiah or Daniel. But while prophets could preach harsh sermons and foretell the future, the primary purpose of the prophetic gift is to interpret circumstances and events in light of God's purposes and declare God's purposes in light of circumstances and events. They are known as mouthpieces of the heart of God.

In the early church, prophets communicated God's Word with the power to prompt life-change in the people who heard them. The authors of Scripture wrote God's revelation with unique prophetic insight, and the documents they produced are foundational for us. God does not inspire prophets to write Scripture or introduce new revelation anymore. Yet Paul urged the entire Corinthian church to seek the gift of prophecy (1 Cor. 14:1), a man named Agabus warned of upcoming events on at least two occasions (Acts 11:27–28; 21:10–14), Philip had four daughters who had prophetic gifts (Acts 21:8–9), and Peter urged those who spoke publicly to do so as if they were declaring the words of God (1 Peter 4:11). However this gift is understood to function (or not) today—and interpretations vary widely—the main point is again the same as with apostles. These leaders do not bear the load of ministry; they equip the church to minister. Any prophetic gifts functioning today are given to clarify and present the truth of Scripture in powerful, culturally relevant ways to call the church into its fullness.

Evangelists. The next leadership gift Paul mentions is evangelists, who have a supernatural ability to share their faith in a way that draws people to Christ. Everyone is called to evangelize in the sense of sharing our faith, but the reference in this verse is to people particularly gifted in evangelistic ministry and able to equip others in it. For those who are not especially gifted as evangelists, our best opportunities to share our faith often come through exercising our other gifts. For example, some practice evangelism through service or hospitality that includes conversations about faith. Evangelists as equippers are able to teach and train believers to do that.

The early church was birthed by apostles, taught under the direction of prophets, and grew as evangelists broadcast the good news. It multiplied as many were converted through the working of these ministry gifts. Many evangelists today continue to spread the message of God's kingdom and draw many to Christ. They lovingly and boldly proclaim the gospel wherever they go and equip the body to share their faith and fulfill the Great Commission to make disciples of all nations (Matt. 28:18–20).

Pastors and teachers. Paul ends this short list with two more ministry gifts, each of which could be treated on its own but are perhaps more familiar to most of us today. Pastors and teachers probably looked a bit different from today's versions of those roles, but they still carried out many of the same functions. Pastor means "shepherd," someone who gives oversight, feeds, cares for, and directs. A teacher communicates the truth of God's Word in a systematic, easily understood way. Together, they counsel and instruct the body of Christ, grounding believers in the truth that helps them grow. They serve in formal roles in churches, seminaries, and ministry organizations, but many also exercise these gifts informally in shepherding and teaching the hearts of God's people. These two gifts may have been applied somewhat differently in New Testament times than they are today, but the point of their mention here is again to emphasize the equipping of every believer.

Why have we taken time to look at each of these ministry gifts and the roles and functions they fulfill? Because they spell out the purpose of leadership in the body of Christ, and leadership is vital to the transformation process. Remember, we aren't talking here about the world's kind of hierarchical leadership. In the body of Christ, "leaders" are meant to come under the people to serve, support, and equip all of its members to do the work of ministry. If we misunderstand the roles given to the renovation team and the work they do best, we will not be able to access the grace they were intended to provide.

In the church today, cultural norms have so skewed the roles of leadership that the average Christian thinks his or her primary responsibility is to come to church, possibly volunteer where needed, and support the pastor or clergy in "the work of the ministry." But if you take that approach, you will miss the very place where God's grace intersects with your heart. You may not grow in the gifts God has given you and fulfill the purposes He has for you because that approach steps back from the Holy Spirit's desire to work powerfully through you and tries to pass it along to the "professionals." This is usually a subconscious, unintentional choice, of course, and it comes from misunderstanding the ministry assignments we just discussed. But as we will see, God's Word sets you up to benefit from those ministries and grow into all you were designed to be.

The Real Purpose of Leadership

Leadership in the church has little to do with prestige or position. The specific purpose of these leadership gifts is to equip the saints (Eph. 4:12)—i.e., all believers.

Most people who have been brought up in the church assume that the pastor's job is to do ministry. Even pastors and other leaders apply that mindset whenever they talk about being "called to ministry" or being trained for "the ministry." Many have learned to qualify those statements with adjectives like "vocational" or "full-time" ministry, but even those don't fully acknowledge every believer's calling to do the work of ministry. This paradigm of professional ministry hinders the true work of the church.

A huge percentage of churches in America—probably somewhere between 80 and 90 percent—have plateaued or are experiencing a decline in attendance. I believe that's because we've lost the picture given to us in Ephesians 4. An average, reasonably energetic pastor can serve the spiritual needs of about seventy-five to one hundred people. Perhaps a high-energy pastor can directly relate to a few more without having a nervous breakdown. And a really driven, obsessive-compulsive pastor can work up to ninety hours a week and deal with two hundred people.

I can say that because I've been there, and it's not the way to go. Every time the phone rang, I would jump. I didn't practice the teaching in Ephesians 4 my first few years as a pastor, even though I had read it many times. I felt like I had to be everything to everyone.

I assumed it was my job to do the ministry—and, to be honest, that perspective is shaped by and supported by many Christians who expect the pastor to be gifted at just about everything and have time for virtually everyone. I didn't realize that this approach was killing me and robbing God's people of the opportunities He wanted to give them to help transform their lives. I lived at a neurotic pace that nearly sacrificed my health. I functioned as a barrier to grace rather than a provider of it.

Can you imagine a general contractor having a team of workers at his disposal but always assuming he'd do a better job on everything that needed to be done? The skills of his team would atrophy, his own work would suffer, and he would burn out before long. Nobody wins at that game. If that's the approach, building projects go slower, people who want to contribute eventually leave, and workmanship wears the signs of stress that went into it.

The leadership roles in church are there "to equip his people for works of service, so that the body of Christ may be built up" (Eph. 4:12). That's how the team is supposed to work. The word "equip" in Greek means "to restore." It's a surgical term for putting a fractured bone back into alignment so it can heal properly. The same word is used for fishermen mending their nets. They "restore" the mesh for usefulness. For a church to be healthy and for transformation to occur, we have to have a restoring, equipping mindset.

The wrong model of ministry is so deeply ingrained in church culture that people new to a biblically functioning equipping church often get frustrated. They find that the pastor isn't accessible to everyone at all times for any reason. In churches I've pastored, we've had to explain our structure to many who question the pastor's absence. "It's not that we don't love you. It's that we love you so much that we're not going to take ministry away from you. We love you so much that even though you think a pastor can do it better, we'll let a layperson who is more gifted and more available serve you as a shepherd." Once that change is in place and grasped by a congregation, members wonder what they were thinking under the old church model. It's a healthier, more effective, and more fulfilling way to do ministry and build up the body of Christ.

This transition can be difficult. Back when I was learning how to equip the saints for ministry rather than doing it all myself, a member called to point out that I hadn't visited her in the hospital. She was in for relatively minor surgery, and she wanted to know why I hadn't come. This was after months of casting a vision for equipping and training small-group leaders with their responsibilities, but old mindsets don't fade away easily. She was having a hard time letting go of the expectation of pastors doing everything and visiting everybody.

I could honestly tell this woman that I didn't know about her surgery, but I knew that would do little to ease her concern. So I asked her, "Are you in a small group?"

"Oh, yes," she said. "They're wonderful!"

"Did anyone from your small group visit?"

"Everyone did. I had visitors every day. They even provided food for days while it was hard for me to get around." She had made her "crisis" known to her group, and they enthusiastically met her need. They also felt it unnecessary to call the pastor about it.

I was both impressed and delighted and made a note to encourage that small group leader. Then I tried to explain what had happened. "Can I tell you something? The body of Christ just operated the way it's supposed to. Those who know you best responded in love and kindness to meet your need. That's what we're trying to accomplish at our church."

She wasn't as impressed as I was. "But you didn't come."

"My job isn't to pastor you. It's to make sure you are pastored well. Your group ministered to you much better than I could have."

We talked a little more about how the group had prayed for her and met her family's needs. We laughed about how much more she enjoyed their cooking than she would have enjoyed mine. But she still couldn't let go of the fact that I hadn't come. The unbiblical model of ministry was deeply ingrained in her—and still is in many others.

If it were humanly possible, I would sit down and have coffee with every member in the congregation after each service. That fits my desires and my gift mix. But believers don't receive the

Equipping everyone for ministry is a model that works.

ministry they need to receive if a few people are doing it all. They also don't provide the ministry they need to provide. Both receiving and providing ministry are vital to growth, and the traditional but unbiblical model of church leadership hinders that process. It puts everything in the contractor's hands and misses out on the craftsmanship of all the specialists who could contribute. With that approach, the transformation doesn't look quite right, and it may not even get finished.

Equipping everyone for ministry is a model that works. In contrast to the conversation I had with the woman who could not envision anything but the traditional model, I was introduced not long afterward to a family of new members who were increasingly involved in the life of the church. I saw the husband's name in ministry reports and knew he was discovering a place of service. But then I heard that he had bypass surgery. I wrote him a note to say I was sorry I was out of town during his surgery but had been praying for him.

I saw him in church the next week—apparently bypass surgery doesn't take nearly as long to recover from as it used to—and he came up to me and said, "Man, what are you doing?"

"What do you mean?" I asked.

"Why are you spending your time writing notes to people like me? I know you love me. My small group was right there with me. My wife and kids are fine. You need to do what God has called you to do. We're happy to care for each other."

He had caught the vision. He understood how the team works together to create the right conditions for change in the lives of its members. I would still visit the hospital sometimes, just as everyone does within their relational network, but usually for the church leadership I was responsible to care for. The church was learning to function according to the model in Ephesians 4, and great things were happening. The transformation of its members—and many other people in the community—looked more like what we see in the New Testament.

2. Every Member Is a Minister

If God has given the church apostles, prophets, evangelists, pastors, and teachers to equip the saints for the work of the ministry, then it stands to reason that the saints are called to minister. Learning God's Word isn't just for the experts. All members are meant to know and understand the revelation He has given us. All members are to develop and hone their life skills and discover and practice their spiritual gifts. All are invited into this life restoration project in order to impart it to others. We are all equipped "for works of service" (v. 12).

The word for "service" is also translated in the New Testament as "ministry." We get the word "deacon" from it. Though many people see "minister" as a synonym for "pastor," they aren't the same at all. The pastor is a type of minister, but ministry involves everyone. Everybody serves. The real action in the body of Christ is getting to see your gifts fitting with the gifts of other believers and watching people's lives change.

Do you remember what Jesus did after defeating Satan? "He took many captives and gave gifts to his people" (v. 8). That means that your spiritual gift is a reminder of your position in Christ. God gives grace not only through the leaders He has called but also through the actions of every other believer using his or her spiritual gifts. Genuine transformation occurs in powerful, supernatural ways when Christians know, understand, and actively use the gifts God has given them.

One of my great delights as a pastor has been in helping people discover and deploy their spiritual gifts. God has given unique supernatural talents to every one of His children, and when we function in them, we experience great joy and others receive what they need to become mature in Christ. (I developed a Bible study resource called *Your Divine Design: How to Discover, Develop, and Deploy Your Spiritual Gifts*, which I believe will be helpful to you. For more information see the back of this book.)

If you've ever played sandlot football, you know what happens in the huddle. The quarterback draws the next play in the dirt. "Charlie, go past the blue car, take a left at the bush, and then go long. Pete, hook around the pothole and stop. Joe, block the big guy." And if every player does his part, the play just might work once in a while.

The huddle is like a gathering place where the team makes its plans, talks about strategy, and gets prepared for the next play. That's what church services are supposed to be like—a spiritual huddle. It isn't where all the action is. It prepares people for the action, which takes place at home, in schools, at the office, on the job site, in community events, and everywhere else people live, work, and play together. Church prepares ministers to do ministry everywhere.

I've served in churches that have a limited number of pastors with very specific duties and thousands of other "full-time" ministers growing, transforming, and helping other people grow and transform. Some of these ministers pose as insurance agents, bus drivers, carpoolers, community activists, tech industry executives, hospitality industry servers, and simply mothers and fathers. The people they live and work with think they're just employees or family members, but they pray with kids on a soccer team, visit the sick, counsel the hurting, lead Bible studies, walk through neighborhoods praying and blessing the homes and inhabitants, worship throughout their day, and display God's love in winsome ways. They are actually ministers of the gospel who shepherd, teach, impart wisdom, express God's heart, and live out their gifts whenever and wherever needed. They are fulfilling God's plan for the church—and being transformed in the process.

When you get involved in the ministering process, life gets exciting. It doesn't matter if you don't know where to start or what your gifts are. In one way or another, you are equipped to help others spiritually, emotionally, physically, and practically. Every believer has at least one spiritual gift because when you believed in Jesus, the Holy Spirit came into your life. You were sealed with the Spirit, adopted into God's family, and forgiven of your sins (Eph. 1:13–14). The Spirit of God now dwells in you, manifesting the power and presence of Jesus. Part of His ministry within you is one or more gifts that will enable you to minister to others.

Discovering and practicing your spiritual gift is an adventure. Plenty of tools are available for discovering and developing your gifts; if you need some direction, ask your church leadership for some resources and direction. But you will only discover your gifts in the context of the body of Christ because that's where and why they are given.

As you learn to serve, care for, and love others by meeting their needs through your spiritual gifts, amazing things will begin to happen. The passage immediately preceding Ephesians 4 gives us a glimpse of them. Paul wrote that God "is able to do immeasurably more than all we ask or imagine, according to his power that is at work within us" (Eph. 3:20). He does the unimaginable through lives that are yielded to Him—that have entered into His death and resurrection by faith, now living as new creations and trusting His power at work in them.

Jesus' words about the attitudes and actions of His followers will describe your experience as you serve. "Give, and it will be given to you. A good measure, pressed down, shaken together and running over, will be poured into your lap. For with the measure you use, it will be measured to you" (Luke 6:38). This verse is often used in sermons about money, but that's not what it's about (though it can apply to financial giving too). It's about ministry. It's an amazing promise for using your spiritual gifts, time, natural talents, and treasure.

3. Ministries Are Developed to Help Believers Live Every Day in Every Way Just as Jesus Would If He Were Living in Their Body

The ultimate goal of equipping the saints for ministry is not just so the saints can do ministry. That's part of it, and every believer is transformed both by doing and receiving ministry in community with each other. But the overarching purpose is "so that the body of Christ may be built up until we all reach unity in the faith and in the knowledge of the Son of God and become mature, attaining to the whole measure of the fullness of Christ" (Eph. 4:12–13). That's God's vision behind the model of every-member ministry.

Verse 13 is packed with implications for us. First, we are being built up in order to reach unity in the faith. This is not just "the faith" in the sense of our common beliefs and ideas about Jesus. It's faith expressed by our unified walk with Jesus, the lives we lead as we carry out the work of ministry.

The second implication is "the knowledge of the Son of God." The Greek word for "knowledge" here is significant. English is one of the few languages in which expressions like "I know you" and "I know algebra" or "I know French" use the same word. In most languages, knowledge of a person (acquaintance, friendship, intimacy) is different from knowledge of facts, concepts, and systems of thought. The word used in verse 13 is *ginosko*, "to know by personal experience." Paul intensified this word with a prefix to make it more powerful: a deep, personal, intimate knowing.

God wants everyone in the body of Christ not only to walk together in faith but to experience Jesus. And that experience leads us to the third implication of verse 13: becoming mature. When you experience Jesus personally in deep, intimate knowledge, you grow. He is your standard of maturity, and the closer you are to Him in relational experience, the more you grow to be like Him. The word for "mature" in this passage is *teleios*, referring to a pattern or design, the end result of where you're headed. In this context, it means you become all you were designed to become as a new creation in Christ.

The last phrase Paul uses in this verse is "attaining to the whole measure of the fullness of Christ." God is committed to your continuing growth. He does not start renovation projects and drop them when they are halfway done. He has called you into abundant life (John 10:10), and He will carry on His work in you to completion (Phil. 1:6). As you trust in the work of His cross and resurrection in burying your old nature and raising you to new life, taking steps of faith and exercising spiritual gifts in community with others, your transformation will continue until you are fully conformed to the blueprint of Jesus.

Along the way, you will want to see how this project is progressing. How do you measure it? How is the design coming together? How is the divine design team working together to reach the common goal? When you're excited about a renovation project, these are questions of anticipation, not of concern or confusion. In the next passage, Paul gives us four specific criteria of transformation into the likeness of Jesus. They are not meant as criticisms; they are encouragements, signs that our transformation is going as planned. When you are living by faith in the head of this project, you will see the evidence. And you can trust that He is masterfully, creatively bringing you toward a beautiful, satisfying result.

CHAPTER 6

How Do You Know If You're Really Changing?

EPHESIANS 4:14-16

Jenn didn't have much trouble making friends. She did, however, have trouble keeping them. She noticed a pattern of making acquaintances, getting closer to people by hanging out, then realizing that her new friends eventually started making excuses, having other commitments, and avoiding time together. At first she would find some fault or flaw in other people that allowed her to place the blame on them. Eventually, she came to the alarming realization that the only common denominator in all these relationships was her.

Finally, Jenn asked one of her estranged friends why they no longer spent any time together. The answer was sobering.

"You kind of use people," her friend told her. "I always felt like I was there to meet your needs, but you were never there for mine. We always talked about you, even when there were important issues going on in my life."

As Jenn thought about it, she realized that as much as this answer bothered her, it was true. She knew she had those tendencies. Her self-centeredness had deep roots, and becoming a Christian as

127

a young adult hadn't uprooted it. No dramatic encounter with God, no miraculous transformation, no wave of a magic wand had made her into a suddenly selfless person. She had gotten a little better with it—at times—but usually she kept defaulting back to her old life, even in new friendships.

If you walk into a room where several toddlers are playing, you probably won't find them supporting each other. You won't over-hear them asking if everybody has enough juice, if anyone needs a diaper change, or if all the others have plenty of toys to play with. They will more likely be focused on their own agenda, competing for the toys they want, and being pretty vocal about whatever they think they need. Their own little worlds are centered on themselves.

You could, however, do or say certain things that would get their attention, like promising a drink or a snack, threatening a punishment, or captivating them with a video or a story. Children redirect their attention often and will believe most of what they're told. They trust their parents to tell them the truth, but they also trust what most other adults tell them. They aren't very discerning, and someone very ignorant or malicious could easily manipulate them or plant deceptive thoughts in their heads. Kids come into this world focused on their immediate needs and having to trust the people around them to care for them and teach them well.

Over time, a lot of things change. Our growing-up years are a process of learning what's true and what isn't, what's right and what's wrong, and what selflessness and relationships are supposed to look like. It's also a time when we shift from mimicking the be-haviors that have been modeled for us and embrace the reason for them in our hearts. We learn how to work hard, how to love well, how to cooperate with others, how to be discerning, and how to respond maturely to the people and situations around us. Granted, many people still struggle with maturity in these areas as adults, but that's often due to a problem in the maturing process of earlier years. Ideally, we become truth-centered, others-centered, and full of integrity as we grow.

You've probably discovered that this is just as true of your life as a believer in Jesus. You probably didn't know much when you were born into His kingdom. It's like entering into a new culture, and it takes time to understand its values, expectations, and ways. Every human being comes from a spiritually fallen and broken background; Paul called it being dead in our transgressions and sins

> *Over time, you have to go through a process of learning what's true, what's right, and what others-centered relationships look like.*

(Eph. 2:1). Life as a new creation is, obviously enough, a new experience. Over time, you have to go through a process of learning what's true, what's right, and what others-centered relationships look like.

That's where the text in Ephesians 4 takes us next. Paul has written about every believer being equipped for ministry so that the whole body of Christ can be built up into unity in the faith, a personal knowledge of Jesus, and the fullness of maturity in Him. But what does that look like? What are the signs of your growth? How can you know if you're really being transformed? In three short verses, we'll see God's litmus test—four characteristics of spiritual maturity.

My Journey of Growth

I didn't know much about the Christian life in my first few months as a believer. The bricklayer who took me under his wing met with me weekly to teach me how to walk with Jesus. Dave was a low-key, low-pressure, genuinely loving guy. I saw how he interacted with his wife and their four children, living out their relationship in Christ as a couple and family. They weren't perfect, but they modeled a marriage that I wanted to have someday.

Dave taught me how to read and study the Bible. He helped me memorize two or three verses a week and introduced me to some classic Christian books. Under his guidance, I learned how to verbalize my faith. I watched him interact with other men across the social spectrum at a Bible study and witnessed their genuine faith and love for one another.

I never enjoyed church much as I was growing up, but now I was eager to get up on Sunday mornings and attend worship. My outward behavior began to change. People told me what a wonderful Christian I was because I was doing all the right activities. They didn't know about all my internal struggles with lust, envy, anger, and coveting, but I looked pretty good on the outside. And I fell into a spiritual trap that almost ruined my relationship with Christ.

What you don't know about transformation can hurt you. All the things we do as part of the spiritual growth process—reading the Bible, prayer, church attendance, small group studies, and so on—are important. Cleaning up outward expressions like profanity and anger outbursts is helpful. But many people will assume that parallel changes are going on internally. As we've seen, transformation is much more than eliminating old activities and taking up new ones. We can sometimes make these outward changes ends in themselves. We call that "legalism"—settling for an appearance of righteousness while our souls are a mass of sinful contradictions. Jesus had harsh words for self-righteous religious people who fit that description. Their hearts were far from God.

I immersed myself in Bible study and Scripture memory over the next two years. I wanted to become the ideal Christian, and plenty of people were encouraging me about how on-fire and deeply spiritual I had become. But beneath the surface, I still had layers of self-righteousness and guilt for not measuring up. I'd beat myself up for missing a quiet time. My prayers turned into lists of needs and requests, and I had to recite them completely before I went to bed. I didn't want to miss church, partly because I felt the need to be noticed there. I became very judgmental of other Christians who were doing less, giving less, and sharing their faith less than I was. My early joy and love for Christ morphed into self-righteous zeal.

Many Christians are living that way today—not intentionally, and unaware of their self-righteousness, but nevertheless filled with a sense of religious duty without much delight in the Lord. They may complain of near exhaustion in their ministry efforts, but they don't exhibit much love or joy. That's what I had become—a joyless, dutiful Christian.

Walking across the campus one day, I ran into a girl who had been a friend for three years. She had seen the changes in my life from my earliest days as a Christian to the person I had become. We stopped to talk, and after exchanging greetings, she caught me off guard with her next words.

"Chip, I remember when you were a really neat guy. When I first met you, you had a contagious joy, and you treated people like they really mattered. You were fun to be around. In fact, you were the first Christian I ever met who I wanted to be like."

I could sense a "but" coming, and I was right. "But that's not you anymore. No matter what people say, you always quote a Bible verse. There's an air about you that makes me feel guilty and bad— like I don't measure up—to you or to God. I don't know what happened to you, but I sure don't like it."

I didn't know what to say, and she didn't expect a response. But she said one more thing before she turned away and left me standing in the autumn sunlight alone. "If this is what it means to be a committed Christian, I don't know that I would ever want to be one."

That caring, non-Christian friend might as well have been an angel. She didn't feel like one at the time—our "chance" encounter seemed like a gut-punch from God designed to maximize the damage to my ego. But her words were a truthful mirror when I desperately needed one.

The whole point of being a Christian isn't to act like one. It's to be one.

I didn't surrender to that truth right away. I immediately began to rationalize her words as unfair, perhaps even jealous, or at least the view of an outsider who just didn't understand. But I couldn't dismiss what she said. Her honesty cut through my defenses. Once I really thought about it, I had to admit she was right. I wasn't very joyful or loving. Under the light of that truth, I began to see all my vain, guilty efforts to gain acceptance from God and fellow Christians through my performance. I had substituted cheap approval for God's genuine love.

The goal of being a new creation is to be transformed from the inside out. The whole point of being a Christian isn't to act like one. It's to *be* one. We aren't supposed to love because we are told to. We are supposed to love because we are loving. Otherwise, we're like a cat trying to act like a dog by barking or a caterpillar trying to fly before having wings. If we find ourselves constantly trying to act against our nature in a certain area, we have not been transformed in that area yet. There is still a gap between the dilapidated house and the new blueprint, between the toddler and the adult. We may be obedient to God in that area—it's better to live obediently than to revert to natural impulses—but the goal is to be transformed so we can live from the new nature we've been given. We have to get to the point where we love, demonstrate patience, give generously, and so on, not because we are supposed to but because it's who we are.

Many people are turned off from Christianity because they've only seen unchanged people trying to act like Christians. They haven't seen many examples of genuine, New Testament transformation. And, to be honest, we may see evidence of both kinds of Christians within us. How can you know whether you are spiritually changing or just going through the motions? When is your behavior the result of religious rules instead of authentic change? How can you tell the difference? Can you really know if you're on the right track?

Four Measures of True Spirituality

If you're being transformed as a new creation into the likeness of Christ, there will be evidence, and much of it is internal. God doesn't leave us in the dark about these things. If He has provided a structure for transformation—leaders equipping, members ministering, and everyone growing together into the likeness of Jesus— He surely wants you to know if you're growing into maturity. Paul addresses this very issue in the next three verses of Ephesians 4.

> Then we will no longer be infants, tossed back and forth by the waves, and blown here and there by every wind of teaching and by the cunning and craftiness of people in their deceitful scheming. Instead, speaking the truth in love, we will grow to become in every respect the mature body of him who is the head, that is, Christ. From him the whole body, joined and held together by every supporting ligament, grows and builds itself up in love, as each part does its work. (Eph. 4:14–16)

This is not just a theoretical or conceptual picture. This model of growth into spiritual maturity produces four discernible results. As you transform into the likeness of Christ, you will be able to see at least these four characteristics at work in your life:

- You can handle Scripture well enough to spot false teachers and trendy religious fads. You maintain doctrinal stability in the face of both.
- You speak the truth in love. Your commitment to relationships allows you to say hard things but in a loving way.
- You fit into the body of Christ with a purpose only you can fulfill. You participate fully, know your gifts, function in those gifts, and bear spiritual fruit.
- Your love for God and others is expanding. When someone asks how you're doing spiritually, your acid test is not the activities you're doing (or not) but the love you have. God measures your spiritual progress by two criteria: whether you are (1) loving God more deeply and (2) loving others more authentically.

Those are four timeless keys to becoming the person you long to be, and they outline God's plan to create an environment in which people grow. If you are part of a local church that practices the four truths that flow out of this passage, you will find authentic transformation occurring in your life. If you begin reacting and responding to people in ways that reflect these principles, you can know God is doing a supernatural work within you.

You'll notice that these signs don't merely measure external activity. Remember, Jesus said our righteousness must surpass the righteousness of the religious leaders of His day (Matt. 5:20), who behaved far more morally and zealously than most Christians do today. Their righteousness emphasized the external, but their Torah reading, synagogue attendance, and frequent praying weren't enough. It's not enough for us to be involved in a church, have a ministry, know the Bible, watch our language, pray daily, memorize some verses, and do all the things good Christians do. That's behavior modification, not Holy Spirit transformation. What we're talking about is a metamorphosis of the heart that grows out of a love relationship with Jesus and is empowered by grace and appropriated by faith. We're growing into adulthood by putting childish mimicry behind us and embracing truth with our hearts.

With that in mind, here are the four pieces of evidence for this grace-empowered, faith-appropriated transformation that results in spiritual maturity.

Doctrinal Stability

You have to have a settled knowledge of God's Word in order to grow. Paul equates being tossed around by various teachings to being spiritual infants (Eph. 4:14). His wording suggests the trickery of someone who manipulates dice—spiritual con men who are exploiting the immature to their own advantage. Growth happens when God's Word forms the foundation of truth for your life. When you become spiritually mature, you know the basic teaching of the Bible. When people knock on your door with a "new truth," you can recognize whether it looks like Jesus or not. When they question fundamental doctrines like the deity of Christ or the Trinity, you can pull out your Bible and say, "Here's what God's Word says." Counterfeit and fraudulent teachings don't suck you in.

That's the first sign of spiritual maturity. That takes more than reading the Bible regularly in order to avoid guilt and check off your to-do list. It isn't just about memorizing facts and reference verses. It's learning and understanding Scripture to make your faith solid and strong, grounded in a clear understanding of your identity in Christ and His work on the cross. You have to know who God is, what Jesus has done to redeem and resurrect you, and who you are in Him. Your transformation is rooted in God's Word.

That begins in your devotional life. Reading the Bible

systematically and regularly should not be a dreaded duty but a highly anticipated occasion, like reading and rereading a love letter that will help you grasp the wonder of your new relationship with Jesus. It's also like learning to wield a razor-sharp sword. Scripture is described in exactly those terms (Heb. 4:12) because it has the supernatural ability to reveal the thoughts and intentions of your heart. Pulling it from its sheath is dangerous at first—you have to know how to use it—but keeping it sheathed is just as dangerous because it leaves you defenseless. It takes time and discipline to accurately grasp Scripture—not just to mentally understand it but to let it sink into the depths of your heart—but if you find a way to read it regularly, think about it, enjoy it, and apply it, it will shape you from within.

I remember reading through the Bible every year using *The Daily Walk Bible*[5] the first ten to fifteen years I was a Christian. It gave me background, context, and an overview of each book. I later read *Know Why You Believe*[6] and *Know What You Believe*[7] by Paul Little and was introduced to basic doctrines and how to answer some hard questions I didn't understand. Today, the YouVersion Bible app and Bible.org are great resources as well.

Remember, reading Scripture is not the goal. It is a means to the goal—cultivating your relationship with Jesus. The more you immerse yourself in it, the easier it becomes. And the more you receive it by faith, the more it stimulates your growth into spiritual maturity.

Authentic Relationships

The second sign of spiritual maturity is increasingly authentic relationships. "Speaking the truth in love, we will grow to become in every respect the mature body of him who is the head, that is, Christ" (v. 15). That reflects a commitment to both people and the truth, and not just when it's convenient. You'll know you're maturing in Christ when you see a fellow Christian moving in a harmful direction and, in spite of how awkward or intimidating it seems, you make time, set up a meeting, and share the truth.

That isn't easy to do. Many people are offended easily, even when you have their best interests in mind. You may get knots in your stomach the night before a necessary conversation and lose a little sleep, but your love is greater than your fear. You can even say that, positioning your words in a framework of love. "I love you too much to stand by in silence when I see how this could affect your marriage." "I really don't want to say anything that would harm our relationship, but I love you too much not to warn you that this situation could cause lasting harm to your kids." Jesus spoke hard words when they were needed, but He had demonstrated a lifestyle of grace and love first, so His hard words carried weight. Be extravagant with your grace and love, and your words will come across the same way. You'll be conforming to the likeness of Jesus.

Being able to speak the truth in love also implies having the maturity to receive the truth in love—and making sure you have people in your life who will tell it to you. After the encounter with my friend on the campus sidewalk, I asked my spiritual mentor if he saw any truth in her words. He confirmed that pride, self-righteousness, and people-pleasing behavior were evident in my life. I was crushed at the time, but I later read a passage that made me see his honesty in a different light. "An open rebuke is better than hidden love! Wounds from a sincere friend are better than many kisses from an enemy" (Prov. 27:5–6 NLT). My mentor had been waiting for the right moment to tell me some of the same things my non-Christian friend pointed out. I realize now that he loved me as few people ever have. He told me what I needed to hear, even at the risk of our relationship.

Do you have many friends like that—people who love you enough to tell you the truth, and whom you love enough to speak with openly and honestly in love? These are mature relationships, and if you can't think of any, start cultivating some of them now. Ask God to help you identify people who may have been speaking the truth in love and coming up against your resistance. Ask Him to reveal anyone who needs to hear truth from you in a spirit of love and grace. Consider how to apply the words of Proverbs 27:5–6 more consistently to those closest to you. Aim for depth in your relationships.

This test of spiritual maturity may be the most neglected sign of transformation in the body of Christ today. The absence of authentic, truth-telling relationships may explain much of the immaturity among professing believers; and being immersed in an individualistic, to-each-their-own, mind-your-own-business culture may explain why these relationships are so absent in the church. Many Christians are living with significant blind spots that undermine their transformation and their relationship with Christ because we have not created an environment of grace and love in which the truth can be told without offending. Spiritual maturity always produces authentic relationships.

Full Participation

The third sign of spiritual maturation is full participation in the body of Christ. As Paul expressed it, "From him the whole body, joined and held together by every supporting ligament, grows and builds itself up in love, as each part does its work" (v. 16). Three critical words in this statement are "whole," "every," and "each." You are one of the "each," an individual part that is designed to fit into the whole. It's possible to worship God in isolation, but personal worship is not the whole Christian life. By yourself, you can't grow spiritually, receive the grace and gifts God imparts through other believers, or impart the grace and gifts He has given to you. You are created to fit with other parts.

The phrase "joined and held together" is a construction term for

two hinged boards. It conveys the idea
of flexible attachment, like ligaments
that connect our bones. The body of
Christ is a beautiful, complex, living
organism, a spiritual renovation project
incorporating many beautiful elements,
and each of us needs to fit together
where God wants us. If you aren't con-

**No amount of
Bible knowledge or
devotional reading
can substitute for
finding your place in
a body of believers.**

nected where God wants you to be connected, the whole body isn't
fitting together. Part of it is, but something significant is missing.
As you mature spiritually, you realize that you depend on the body,
and the body depends on you. You participate fully.

No amount of Bible knowledge or devotional reading can substitute for finding your place in a body of believers. It is vital in your life
in Christ to get connected with a local expression of Christ's body—
loving and being loved in a way that's a good fit with all concerned.
God is love (1 John 4:8, 16), which means He is relational by nature.
You cannot become like Him if you are not regularly in a position
of expressing and receiving love with other believers. Even if you are
extremely introverted and less relational than others, this dimension
of spiritual growth must be present somewhere in your life. Service
of any kind is a great place to begin, but eventually you will discover
the gifts and talents that you most need to give, as well as those you
most need to receive from others. Teaming up with other believers
enables you to be "joined and held together" as God designed.

As a pastor, I used to tell our church that the most loved people
there were those involved in ministry—not because we loved others
less, but because those who were relationally connected experienced
love from many directions and felt accepted as part of the body. As
you team up for ministry with other believers, you learn to pray and
share honestly with each other and discover that you share many of

the same struggles. You get your eyes off your own needs and see the needs of others, and they see yours. Genuine participation leads to the highest and clearest evidence of transformation: love.

A Growing Capacity for Love

The last half of verse 16 describes an increasing love among believers. The body of Christ "grows and builds itself up in love, as each part does its work." This is God's kind of love, of course—the kind that speaks honest and difficult words when necessary, that sacrifices one's own needs for the sake of others, that seeks the best for everyone whenever possible. Emotional responses of love are wonderful and can be very godly (see Paul's affection in Philippians 1:9), but love is not *only* emotional. We know we are maturing spiritually when we see evidence in ourselves of the supernatural love Jesus modeled for us.

I've seen new believers embrace this kind of love very quickly and older believers who are still very much focused on themselves. But if we are maturing in Christ, we generally move from self-focused to other-focused as we are being transformed into His image. Our capacity to love is not dependent on the "right" environment. I know people in difficult marriages or parenting relationships who have balanced truth and love admirably without growing bitter. I've received letters from people who are battling cancer and facing the end of their lives but still very much focused on the needs and concerns of the people around them. They could be completely preoccupied with their own problems, but instead they share their faith with hospital staff, call to check on how other people are doing, take care of their families to whatever degree they are able, and see their painful journey as something either decreed or allowed by God that can only work out for their good (Rom. 8:28). They have grown in their capacity to love.

I will never forget the first time I witnessed this kind of love as a new Christian. It was in a small college ministry with a few young professionals in West Virginia. We met in a living room off campus, did small discipleship groups throughout the week, and saw God work in powerful ways. I felt like I was part of a family that really loved one another and would do anything for each other. One member's family was in a tragic accident, and we began to pray about the huge financial need that resulted. The money was given by someone in the group, no strings attached, and without mention of their name. I inadvertently learned later that one of the young professionals had emptied her entire retirement account to meet the need. I had never seen that kind of sacrifice or love before, and it recalibrated my perspective of what it means to be a part of the body of Christ.

More recently, my wife, Theresa, and I were having dinner with a couple and sharing the ups and downs in our lives. It was the first time we had eaten at a restaurant in nearly six months during the coronavirus pandemic, so I asked them how they were holding up. I knew they were compassionate and committed followers of Jesus because, in addition to their three kids, they had adopted four children from around the world, two of whom had Down syndrome. But as the evening went on, Don shared about being in a Bible study and hearing about a very close friend of one of the members who was going to die unless he got a new kidney. As their small group prayed week after week for this friend, Don was prompted to go through the testing to give his kidney if it was a match. He had just learned that day that he was not a match, and he was deeply saddened that he couldn't give up one of his kidneys to extend that man's life. That's serious love and commitment.

This is the kind of love that changes the world. This is what Jesus talked about when He said, "Greater love has no one than this: to lay down one's life for one's friends" (John 15:13). Love is more than having a warm feeling toward fellow Christians, attending church, or even joining a small group and being nice to one another. The kind of love that changes the world is what the Holy Spirit produces in us as He matures us and transforms us into the image of Christ.

In fact, if we are trusting in and relying on God's Spirit at work within us, we often find that crises are great catalysts for our capacity to love. They put us into a position of having to choose between a victim mentality and a new creation mentality. Supernatural, outward-directed, sacrificial love—what the Bible calls *agape*—is a reflection of God's nature within us. It is transforming not only for ourselves but also for those around us.

You can know how well you're doing in your journey with Christ not by how diligent you are with your spiritual to-do lists but by honestly answering a two-part question: *Am I loving God more deeply as evidenced by my conformity to His will* (John 14:21) and *am I loving others more authentically* (Rom. 12:9)? The degree to which you can answer those questions positively is the degree to which the Holy Spirit is doing the miraculous work of transformation within you.

Warning! Be Careful How You Handle the Evidence

There are risks in trying to measure your degree of spiritual growth. For one thing, it can turn you inward to focus on yourself. There are healthy forms of introspection, but they are usually brief, honest, and redemptive. Constantly gazing at your progress is not healthy and very often results in self-criticism and guilt. Don't go there. Occasionally check to see if you are exhibiting inward growth and not just outward appearances, but then turn outward again. Your growth depends on your outward-focused love.

Trying to measure your growth can also raise questions of how much is enough and prompt you to dismiss all of your motives even when some good ones are mixed in with the bad. God gives you a lot of grace. Agree with Him on that and give yourself plenty of grace too. This is not a pass-fail proposition. It's a growth process, often incremental, with steps forward, backward, sideways, and forward again. That's okay. As long as you are moving in the right direction over time, you are on the right track. Think of it a lot more like becoming best friends and evaluate your trust, connection, and loyalty to one another, not like a student checking your report card from the teacher.

Above all, remember that the measures of spiritual maturity are never meant to be a crushing weight to produce guilt and shame, and they are never a basis for comparing ourselves with others. They are offered as a light to help us follow the promptings of the Holy Spirit as He works within us to make us into the people we long to become and were designed to be. They are reminders not of how we've failed but of who we are becoming.

God is committed to helping you become the person He created you to be. He has made you new on the basis of Jesus' crucifixion and resurrection, given you spiritual gifts, provided leaders to equip you, and called you into the fellowship of believers to live, love, serve, and enjoy His presence together. His goal is not for people to notice how spiritual you are or be impressed with your disciplines. He wants people to look at you and think, *He/she used to be so angry, so self-centered, so controlling, so negative, so codependent, so addicted, so stuck . . . but now, look at the change!* He wants your life to be the evidence of supernatural transformation.

That doesn't mean you should kick yourself for every stumble, every imperfection, or every step backward—even if they are really big and noticeable. God's mercies are new *every* morning. You aren't merely a new creation who becomes old again over time. You are constantly, always new. The question is not whether you've arrived. It's whether you're moving forward. Every day you grow to be more like Jesus—or notice that you're not and correct your course— you're growing into the spiritual adult you were called to be.

God longs to bring out the best in His children, and that takes time. But with that goal in mind, it's important to ask yourself a very important question from time to time: *Am I positioning myself in an environment where God can change me?* If you don't know how to answer that, revisit the diagnostic questions at the end of chapter 1. You may even notice some progress between the first time you read them and now. But even if you don't, you now have more context for answering them. Consider them carefully, not with a self-condemning attitude, but with a heart for real change. The more you bring your longing for change to God, the more you will begin to see your areas of needed growth. And you will notice areas where you have already grown, like an increasing awareness of truth, a deepening of relationships, an increasing capacity to love, and a strong sense of putting childish things behind and maturing into the person God designed you to be.

CHAPTER 7

How Do You Break Out of a Destructive Lifestyle?

EPHESIANS 4:17–24

I t's a scene that plays out over and over again. I'm having a conversation with someone, and once we've gotten past the casual introductions and into some deeper spiritual issues, the throat-clearing begins. My conversation partner looks around as if about to divulge a threat to national security and begins to share a private battle he or she has been waging unsuccessfully for years. These people are often leaders in churches and pillars in the community, and despite appearing to have it all together have shared secret sexual addictions, eating disorders, affairs, habitual outbursts of anger, and resentment and bitterness dating back decades. To be fair, they've also seen Christ change their lives dramatically in many ways . . . except for this private stronghold. Overwhelmed with guilt and shame, the real question they are asking is, "How do I live a holy life? How can I break out of this habitual pattern of sin and destruction?"

I get it. We can be completely sincere in our personal salvation, experience joy and peace, and develop new desires—including a longing to be holy—and still begin to wonder, even after decades, what's wrong. Sometimes, after years of failure in a specific area, people begin to question whether their salvation was genuine.

A caterpillar's metamorphosis into a butterfly is a genuine, miraculous change, but it isn't a sudden one. Some miracles happen so slowly that we can't really see them well without watching the highlights at high speed. But that doesn't make them any less miraculous. The caterpillar wraps itself in a fine thread that forms a cocoon and waits. Eventually, the cocoon splits, a new creature emerges—dark, wet, quivering, and hardly looking beautiful—and with great difficulty unfolds its wings. Dazzling patterns and colors appear. Fragile legs begin to move. And before long, it takes flight, dancing in the wind.

Somehow, a creature that crawls has become a creature that flies. Like a seed in the ground, the worm seems to die before it emerges as something different and new. It takes on a completely different nature.

That's a great picture of our spiritual metamorphosis. If we aren't watching it in time-lapse images, it may seem excruciatingly slow. And at first appearances, our transformation may not seem like much of a transformation at all. The exchange of old for new happens imperceptibly within the cocoon, and we appear fragile when we first come out. But with seemingly great difficulty, our struggle to break out of the cocoon and spread our wings eventually leads to fluttering and soaring freely and beautifully in spring breezes and the summer sun.

New and old Christians often ask why this transformation doesn't seem as radical and liberating as they expected. How can we live genuinely holy lives, inside and out? Why does it take so long? And why, if we're empowered by the Holy Spirit, does it seem so difficult?

We'll explore some of those questions in this chapter, but the answers will go back to how we see God, how we see ourselves, and whether we actually believe the promises He has given us. One of the biggest problems believers face is that when we emerge from our cocoon in rebirth, we still tend to see ourselves as worms. Some theologies continue to stress our wormlike nature as sinners and never really move on to discussing the divine nature we've received and the resurrection we can now experience. We have trouble grasping our new identity because our only experience is with the old one. So Scripture spells it out for us, repeatedly pointing us to Jesus. That's what a new creation looks like. And when we really begin to grasp that—and fill our vision with who He is rather than who we used to be—we begin to spread our wings and fly.

Why Is This New Life So Difficult?

I completely understand those awkward conversations and how to live a holy life. I've wrestled with the same guilt and frustration. But in order to live a holy life, we need to recognize that we all bring the baggage of our old destructive lifestyles with us when we come to Jesus, and it doesn't just go away. But though the struggles are normal, God has provided a way of deliverance.

Part of the problem is how we define "holy." Some people think it means you become a super-saint with hyper-morality who knows every Bible verse relevant to every situation, spends hours in prayer, never has a bad day, and carries an aura of supernatural presence. And while Bible verses, prayer, and the presence of God are wonderful, holiness simply means being set apart for special service—becoming winsome and loving, being transformed bit by bit over time into the likeness of Jesus. God understands our ups and downs, forward and backward steps, and our struggles and frustrations. The sanctification process is not neat and clean. But over time, as we learn to cooperate with His Spirit within us, He changes our thoughts, actions, attitudes, and words. The love of Christ moves us to become more holy and whole.

This process has far too often been oversimplified and over-spiritualized. Some sermons and books make it seem easy and automatic. But both the Bible and nature give us a picture of a metamorphosis filled with struggle and tension. The grace that saved us is the grace that empowers us to say no to worldliness and ungodliness (Titus 2:12). It gives us a bigger "yes" to God. It isn't easy to live a pure life in a sinful world, but it is possible. God has given us all we need to do it.

Like the butterfly coming out of its cocoon, there is tension and struggle in our transformation, just as there is also beauty and wonder in it. But can you imagine a new butterfly looking back toward the cocoon and reminiscing about the safety and security it felt there? And then looking at its wings and wondering if they're really going to hold up? And looking back toward all of its worm buddies and wishing it could inch along with the crowd like it used to? The idea of a brand-new life isn't all fun and adventure. It can be as intimidating as it is exciting. Is the faith that saved us really going to work in day-to-day life and the crises we face? Can we really put ourselves out on a limb to pray with confidence? And what about our past friendships? Now that we're new, what happens to everything old?

A new life demands a new lifestyle.

As unsettling as the unknown can be, our only calling now is to live in the newness we've been given. That does have consequences for old ways, old attitudes, and old relationships. Fallen human nature tends to cling to the familiarity and security of the known, even when it is unsatisfying. Our new nature must embrace what seems unknown to us, even though we've been told much about it, because it is far better than anything we've experienced. We are called to fly into the adventure.

If you're trying to figure out how to live as a Christian while clinging to the security of your cocoon, you are going to struggle. A new life demands a new lifestyle. That's the key to understanding growth and holiness. To paraphrase the beautiful statement in 2 Corinthians 5:7 about becoming a new creation, you are no longer a worm. You're a butterfly. Old things are gone. All you have is the new.

Two Spiritual Pitfalls

Throughout the Christian era, believers have struggled with two errors in trying to live holy lives, two deadly cliffs on each side of the road, both of which lead to brokenness. We come out of sin-dominated pasts—guilt, shame, pain, dysfunction, addictions, character flaws, distorted desires, and much more. As much as we want to sever those strings, they will remain attached until we learn to avoid the errors on the right and the left of our journey.

Moralism

The first pitfall is moralism. It shows up in well-meaning church people who understand that moral purity is a priority. In trying to get people to live like Christians, they distort what the Bible says about grace, and to prevent abuses of grace, they teach, implicitly or explicitly, that God loves those who keep certain rules and is down on those who don't. The people who keep the right rules are therefore pure and holy. Their moralizing creates a new set of laws.

New believers often hear, "Now that you're a Christian, you need to do this, this, and this, and you need to stop doing this, this, and this . . ." The rules may vary from group to group, but they all focus on externals—spiritual behaviors like Bible reading and prayer, daily behaviors like eating, drinking, clothing, entertainment, and so on. And the results are disastrous. By emphasizing the outward signs of transformation, they are missing its inward essence.

Before long, Christian shoulders are crushed by the weight of all the dos and don'ts. While Jesus said those who love Him will keep His commandments (John 14:15), most moralistic rules have little to do with His commandments, which focus on love and internal change. Before long, people feel guilty, frustrated, tired, and convinced they will never measure up. They start to fake it, think about walking away, or just live in despair.

The most strong-willed rule-keepers eventually become like the Pharisees of Jesus' day—the moral, upright citizens of Jewish society. They appear spiritual, but their faith in their ability to keep the rules translates into self-righteousness and moralizing judgments. They seem to have overcome all negative, sinful thoughts, even as sins like pride, lust, and anger play out in their hearts. After smothering so many other people, their moralism eventually smothers them too.

New Christians who follow such teaching begin with joy and peace but soon degenerate into joylessness. There's no room for error or adventure on this path, and eventually there is no room for Christ. The beauty and delight of their relationship with God turns into dry and mechanical servitude. Grace-filled wonder turns to drudgery. It's suffocating.

Antinomianism

The other pitfall is antinomianism. The word means "against law," as in opposition to the laws and rules of moralists. People who fit into this group begin with the same observation moralists do— that many Christians are not living like Christians—but come to a very different conclusion. They look at rules and say, "That's not what the Christian life is about. It's about relationship, not regulations. It's a gospel of grace and freedom. God isn't hung up on your behavior."

Even in the New Testament era, groups of antinomians emphasized being saved by grace. They were exactly right on that point. It
really is a gospel of grace and freedom. But they took Paul's teaching
about being out from under the old law and lived it in the extreme.
They dispensed with all standards and even twisted their freedom
to mean that the more they sinned, the more they could experience
God's grace (see Rom. 5:20 and Paul's response in 6:1–4) They per-
verted grace like the moralists, but in an opposite direction.

Antinomians believe, very correctly, that God does not love us
according to our performance and, because salvation is a gift from
God, we're going to heaven regardless of what we do. But their conclusion is wrong. They give license to lustful passions in the name
of grace and freedom. But that brand of freedom simply leads back
into the bondage of old, enslaving desires.

Paul addressed antinomians in several letters. He agreed that
we are called to freedom, but urged, "Do not use your freedom to
indulge the flesh; rather, serve one another humbly in love" (Gal.
5:13). We may be free from the Old Testament law, but we are called
to a higher and deeper standard, the law of love. We can't simply
rationalize the call to conform to God's character away.

Then What's the Answer?

Nearly every Christian has struggled with this dilemma. If we don't
become holy by keeping standards and rules, and we aren't called
to dismiss them, what's left? If one dangerous cliff leads to self-
righteousness and the other dangerous cliff leads to no practical
righteousness at all, how do we become holy?

If we put this dilemma into our metamorphosis metaphor, the
caterpillar would be wondering, *If trying to apply butterfly behavior
to my life doesn't really make me a butterfly, and if letting go of all
butterfly expectations leaves me living like a caterpillar, what do I do?*

The answer is to actually be a butterfly. That's what we've been discussing in this book: inward change that leads to outward change. The goal is for us to become so inwardly transformed that we no longer have to live a Christian life that goes against our natural grain. Righteousness becomes written on our hearts so we don't try hard to live it out or dismiss it as legalism. We put the blueprint of Jesus before us, gaze at the beauty of His character, and start walking in that direction. Old passions begin to fall away as new passions fill our hearts. If that isn't happening, we are like butterflies looking back at the cocoon and life on the ground, forgetting the skies above.

God doesn't call us to try harder (moralism) or to pray a prayer and continue living the way we did, knowing that grace covers it all (antinomianism). He calls us to proactively put away our old life and set our focus on knowing and seeing Christ accurately, "being transformed into his image with ever-increasing glory" (2 Cor. 3:18). Just as a kid starts to take on the mannerisms and style of a favorite athlete or entertainer simply from watching and wanting to be like that celebrity, we become like Jesus as we get glimpses of what He's really like and how much He loves us. We put on our new selves as if they were the wings of a butterfly. And that's exactly where Paul takes us next in our journey through Ephesians 4.

So I tell you this, and insist on it in the Lord, that you must no longer live as the Gentiles do, in the futility of their thinking. They are darkened in their understanding and separated from the life of God because of the ignorance that is in them due to the hardening of their hearts. Having lost all sensitivity, they have given themselves over to sensuality so as to indulge in every kind of impurity, and they are full of greed.

That, however, is not the way of life you learned when you heard about Christ and were taught in him in accordance with the truth that is in Jesus. You were taught, with regard to your former way of life, to put off your old self, which is being corrupted by its deceitful desires; to be made new in the attitude of your minds; and to put on the new self, created to be like God in true righteousness and holiness. (Eph. 4:17–24)

Paul uses very strong language to issue a challenge: "I tell you this, and insist on it in the Lord." The challenge is for Gentiles who have converted to Christianity out of pagan backgrounds to no longer live the way they once did. Ephesus was a center of religious tourism and was a mixed bag of cultural and moral standards. Devotion to Greek and Roman gods involved rituals but rarely any moral changes. Paul calls that way of life darkened, ignorant, hardened, sensual, impure, and greedy—the same words many people use to describe modern society. He says this way of thinking is futile—vain, aimless, purposeless, and detached from God. None of these descriptions fit the Christian life.

Then comes the sharp contrast. This is "not the way of life you learned" as a believer in Jesus (v. 20). New Christians, spiritually reborn, were told from the start that a radical life-change was part of the process and that they would have to count the cost. Paul is reminding them of their new nature. Encountering Jesus isn't like meeting anyone else. The results are transforming.

Apparently, some of the Ephesians were falling back into old, immoral ways. Paul reminds them that they were taught to put away the old self, which is being corrupted by deceitful desires, and put on the new self, which comes with a new mental attitude (vv. 22–24). The picture he presents is of taking off old clothes and putting on new ones, like someone entering a new culture and wanting to dress the part or a caterpillar being transformed inside its cocoon. New believers may not recognize their transformation yet, but it's there. And it should look a lot like the "true righteousness and holiness" of God (v. 24).

The Inner Anatomy of Change

Three major points about our inward transformation become clear in Paul's instructions in this passage. He essentially dissects the process of having God's righteousness written on our hearts. The first two emphasize the reasons for a holy life. The third tells us how to live in it.

1. Believers Must Lead Lives Progressively Characterized by Moral Purity

Moral purity is never meant to be an option for a Christian. We are supposed to live differently—not in order to earn God's favor (moralism) but because of who we are and whose we are. We have a new identity, we have been changed, and we belong not to the world but to God.

That's Paul's rationale for his challenge to stop living as the Gentiles do. Their darkened understanding is futile, and they are separated from God through ignorance and hardened hearts. They have lost all sensitivity, have given themselves over to sensuality, indulge in impurity, and constantly lust for more (vv. 17–19). They can't think themselves out of their predicament. They are mentally and spiritually blind, not through intellectual ignorance but through moral ignorance. They are like petrified wood before God—rocks that have no life and cannot feel.

That's why children more readily receive the message about God and His goodness. They still have soft hearts. But that fallenness within each of us turns us toward me, my, and mine as the center of our own little universe. We miss God's presence. Our hearts harden. We become calloused and insensitive, morally ignorant and confused, inevitably falling short of His glory (Rom. 3:23). In this section of Ephesians, Paul strongly urges all believers—he's talking to God's people here—*Don't live this way!*

Paul's descriptions of his world should sound familiar. We also live in a morally confused society. No one has to go looking for temptation. It comes to each us—at work, in entertainment, through the screens of our devices, and almost everywhere we turn. Shame and remorse are out of style. Many have surrendered to their passions with gusto and continually lust for more. We have plenty of examples in our world of what happens when people reject God.

This rejection of God and truth is a subtle and gradual process. The more people indulge their sins, the more they become calloused to the Holy Spirit's conviction and sin's consequences. Like an addict who gets a thrill from the first hit but needs more and more to keep the thrill alive, the people Paul describes in verses 17–19 keep giving in to the power of sin until they are consumed and can feel and reason no more. It's a slow, deceptive process, and we've all wrestled with it somehow and felt that pull. Paul's words pull us back out and into the light of the new creation.

This downward slide can happen in any area of life. Successful businesspeople have told me how they had everything—nice homes, vacation condos, expensive cars, all of life's luxuries—and lost their family and relationships in the process. They confide that they lied to themselves every step of the way. That's what Paul is warning against—self-serving, obsessive, addictive, sinful lifestyles. He calls God's people out. A new life demands a new lifestyle.

2. An Immoral Lifestyle Is Inconceivable for Believers

Holiness is about wholeness. God wants to save us from destructive patterns that break His heart, reflect badly on His family, and destroy us. His standards aren't random. They protect us from ourselves.

If we don't turn decisively from sin and embrace our calling, we will err on the side of wrong, rationalizing and compromising our sin. Imagine verbalizing what our behavior often says: "Lord, it's just a little immorality." "Can I covet in moderation?" "Are You okay with reasonable dishonesty, as long as no one gets hurt?" We easily see through these questions, but many of us, me included, have lived through long periods of tolerating a little immorality, dishonesty, and coveting in our hearts. But Scripture leaves us no room to negotiate with God about our spiritual purity.

Your motivation for a holy life is not to earn brownie points with God.

Paul reminds us that we did not come to know Christ that way. We were taught according to the truth that is in Jesus (vv. 20–21)—what believers had heard about His teachings and the life He lived, the perfection He demonstrated, the love and peace He displayed. We chose to follow Him, to conform to His nature. So an immoral lifestyle is inconceivable for us for two reasons: (1) it contradicts who we are; and (2) it contradicts who Christ is.

Your motivation for a holy life is not to earn brownie points with God. As a saved, forgiven, cleansed believer, you are loved right now as much as you could ever be loved—infinitely and eternally, regardless of your performance. That's your motivation. You don't live a holy life in order to attain your new identity. You live a holy life *because of* your new identity. You are now holy, set apart for Him, regardless of old habits and inclinations. A good moral life is simply the byproduct and reflection of a genuine, loving relationship with God. He loves you and manifests His character through you, producing peace and joy in your heart and in your relationships with others. You get a taste of heaven on earth because that's consistent with who you are now and with who Christ is.

As long as the thought behind your motivation is, "God loves me when I'm good and is down on me when I'm bad," you will live a very frustrating, unproductive life in guilt or self-righteousness. And you will have missed the wonder, beauty, and joy of the relationship along the way.

3. We Experience Personal Purity by Following God's Threefold Principles of Transformation

The reasons for personal holiness are strong motivations, but they still don't tell us how it happens. How do we win the battle when we struggle with secret desires, are tempted to go to sites we shouldn't go to, track the stock market obsessively as if our well-being depends on it, spew out sarcasm and destructive comments, or face whatever other temptations and addictions confront us? How can deeply flawed people in desperate situations live as God has called us? Paul gives us three principles of holy transformation in verses 22–24.

Put off the old self. The old self is corrupted by deceitful desires, and Paul uses a metaphor to tell us what to do with it: "Take off the ragged and shabby clothes of your old life. Quit wearing that old cocoon like a coat and cast it aside" (see v. 22). He does not present this as a gradual process. It's decisive, a point in time. Our actual transformation may play out over time, but it's important to make a clear decision rather than waffling back and forth between old and new. Draw a line between your new and old self and determine not to go back across it. Whatever temptations tripped you up before—images, bars, relationships, addictions, lusts, greed—don't entertain them anymore. The first step of holiness is turning away from your old life. It's an intentional decision to leave it behind.

If you don't, you'll remain in a vicious, self-destructive cycle that will eat you up inside. I know that from experience. I spent the first couple of years straddling the fence. I was singing praises

to God on Thursday nights and barhopping with basketball teammates on Friday and Saturday nights. I believe the most miserable
people on earth are genuine believers who continue to live in known
sin—who try to live a double life, longing for God's best while sab-
otaging themselves with spiritually harmful habits. Guilt and shame
eat away at them, destroying their peace and joy. It's like drinking
poison that tastes good and expecting the taste to overcome the ef-
fects. They live in no-man's-land—unable to enjoy sin because of the
Holy Spirit within them, unwilling to leave it because old habits and
temptations die hard.

That pretty much described my life. Guilt and shame were constant companions, interrupted by heartfelt confessions and promises I didn't keep. My prayers seemed pointless. My fellowship with
God suffered. The effect of His Word dulled. And I eventually realized the double life wasn't worth it.

If you've ever been there—or are there right now—you've also
probably realized it isn't worth it. You know the pain it can cause—
overwhelming guilt, feeling trapped, desperate for something to
change. God loves you too much to leave you there.

Let me speak the truth in love here: the consequences of your
sins will continue to multiply and cause pain to you and others. If
the Spirit of God is telling you to put your old life behind, make
a hard-and-fast decision to leave the cocoon and move forward
fully into your new identity. Whatever your old clothes are—
materialism, sexual impurity, self-centeredness, anger, bitterness,
greed, status-seeking—don't try to put them in the laundry. Take
them off and throw them away like rags. Ask the Holy Spirit to
search your heart and put His finger on anything that needs to go.
He wants to heal, forgive, and clothe you in the royal robes of His
kingdom. Be as drastic as you need to be to address whatever has
enslaved you and will continue to tempt you back into your old life.

Be made new in the attitude of your mind. The present tense of this command implies a continual process. If your mind were a computer, putting off the old would be like placing all your unwanted files in a folder and deleting it. Being made new would be like discovering spiritual software called "Walking with Christ" and installing it. But you have to give it continual input—Scripture reading, positive spiritual relationships with other believers, grace imparted through their gifts, accountability in the fellowship, and whatever it takes to make the most of this amazing new software. You don't have to forsake all your old friends, but Scripture is clear that you become like those who you spend the most time with. Maintain your old friendships, if possible, but change where and when you hang out together. Build true friendship around times, places, and other people that don't pull you back into your old lifestyle. Stop inputting bad data into your life. It may take time, but program your heart and mind with the truth and relationships of God's agenda for you.

Make holy transformation the default setting of your mind. Prioritize your life around being like Jesus, not just in imitation but in letting His Spirit rise up within you. Talk with God frequently and in depth. Practice purity. Choose integrity and love. Spend time with people who are headed in the same direction; a few traveling companions can make all the difference. Always have this software and its default settings open and running. As Paul urged in Colossians 3:17, do everything as a representative of Jesus. You'll find your entire orientation increasingly directed by the Holy Spirit.

Put on the new self. God has given you new clothes—the wardrobe of Jesus Himself. Just as putting off the old self involves a willful decision, putting on the new self is a choice to focus on becoming a man or woman of God. Your relationship with Christ becomes central to all you are and do. You consciously aim to reflect Jesus in your lifestyle, thoughts, feelings, work ethic and relationships, your marriage or singleness, your family relationships, your friendships, your hobbies and activities, your politics, your investments of time and money, and everything else you do.

Not long after becoming a Christian, I made some drastic decisions to break with my old life and put on the new. They don't seem like major changes now, but they were the biggest steps of my life at the time. They got me off the fence and planted my feet in the land of personal purity and integrity. Transformation doesn't just happen; it often comes through sudden decisions and in the midst of crises.

One of my decisions involved treating the opposite sex in a way that would honor God. Girls outnumbered guys four to one at the college I attended in the early '70s, the height of the sexual revolution, and I realized my mind was overwhelmed by temptations. My thoughts and relationships were not very healthy. So I made some very practical decisions to break with the past and put on the new self. I stopped eating at the cafeteria on the first floor of the girls' dorm, removing myself from a position of sitting with fellow teammates and "evaluating" several hundred girls walking by my table three times a day. I also began memorizing Scripture in my battle with lust and impure thoughts.

I didn't know anything about renewing my mind at the time, but my roommate was headed to a Christian training program for the summer and had to memorize sixty key Bible verses in The Navigators's Topical Memory System prior to leaving. Since we were competitive about everything, I copied down the sixty verses and decided I would memorize them all before he did. I put them on little cards and carried them with me everywhere, reviewing daily in classes, on the way to baseball practice, before I went to bed, and any time in between. I was committed to showing him I was better and faster at memorizing verses—not exactly Christlike motives.

One day, I met a very attractive girl in our college ministry, and we talked outside the library for about fifteen minutes. As I walked away, I had a sudden realization. My eyes had been focused on her eyes the whole time, and I had no impure thoughts. This was a major breakthrough, and I didn't understand it, but I still remember that it was day twenty-one and I had memorized twenty-one verses. My desires started to change, and I experienced a new joy. I had put away the old, began renewing my mind with God's Word, and put on a new attitude that honored Him. Miraculously, my desires changed as I renewed my mind, and I developed refreshing, healthy friendships with sisters in Christ. I no longer felt marked by failure, defeat, and guilt.

I also broke off some relationships and practices that had been dragging me down. I rationalized my barhopping with non-Christian friends by telling myself I was helping them come to Christ. But I realized I was the one being affected. I made a decision, stuck with it, and replaced that habit with positive activities and relationships on Fridays. I discovered what I had been missing—new interactions and positive experiences helping others. I began to see even more possibilities and benefits to this idea of holy transformation. I actually felt that I was experiencing abundant life as Jesus promised.

So what about you? What old habits or practices do you need to take off? What specific ways do you need to renew your mind?

These were big steps for me, but only the beginning of transformation. That process never ends. Three years later in seminary, God brought about another major step of transformation.

Grace, and Then . . .

About six years after I became a Christian, several of us seminary students were given the opportunity to have regular brown-bag lunches with Dr. Howard Hendricks. We talked about our dreams, struggles, questions, goals, priorities, schedules, planning, discipline, and all the other life issues we could imagine. Dr. Hendricks usually let us ramble, but I still remember him bringing the conversation to a standstill one day with his commanding voice.

"Look, guys," he said. "You've got to get this. It's grace! From beginning to end, the Christian life is grace."

Most of us were driven, high-performance personalities, and our conversation had been almost entirely about the great impact we would make and the great things we would do for God.

> "There's nothing you can do that will cause God to love you any less than He does right now."

"Men," he continued, "there are two things you must understand. Number one, there's nothing you can do to make God love you any more than He does right now. Number two, there's nothing you can do that will cause God to love you any less than He does right now. So get this down, gentlemen. You are loved by God right where you are today as much as He will ever love you. What you do has nothing to do with how loved you are. You got that?"

We got it. It's still imprinted on my mind.

Then Dr. Hendricks went to the blackboard and wrote four words boldly: **Objectives**, **Priorities**, **Schedule**, and **Discipline**. "Men, I've been around ministries and people in the marketplace all over the world for thirty years. Here's what I've learned. Once you clearly grasp that central fact that it's all by grace, you can also see that grace doesn't mean you do nothing. Grace means that based on God's great love, you spend the rest of your life expressing your thanks and love for Him, not earning His favor. You live a life by His power that is wholly pleasing to Him. Now, let me show you how that works."

He walked back to where he started writing. "First, what's your OBJECTIVE? If it's to be rich, that's what you'll go for. Is it to be famous? That's what you'll go for. If you want to know Christ, you need to write at the top of your list, 'I want to be a man of God.' That's your objective."

We nodded.

"Do you know where that'll take you? Nowhere. You've got to have a plan that makes that your number one PRIORITY," he said, pointing to the second word. "How are you going to get there? What's your plan to become a man of God? What's it going to take? Objectives determine behavior. If you really want to be a man of God, you've got to develop a clear-cut plan to get there. What will it mean in terms of time in the Word of God? How will your objective determine the other books you read, or what you choose to do or choose not to do—not because you think you have to or to gain brownie points with God, but because by His grace you want to be all He wants you to be? What's it going to cost in your gut and your heart to be a man of God?"

Dr. Hendricks pointed at the first term again. "There's your target, your objective. Then you have to come up with a plan that will make it your number one priority. Once that's in motion, you've got to make your plan a part of your SCHEDULE. Becoming a man of God has to show up on your schedule. Many people have a great plan to meet God every morning, but the plan doesn't mean much if it isn't put into action. You don't say, 'I don't have time to meet with God.' Are you kidding me? He created everything. You start your day with Him. And then you plan in when you're going to read. And you plan in how you're going to be in a small group, and you make sure your plan includes your roles with your family. The man of God will be a man of God for his wife and kids . . . not just in the pulpit."

Finally, he said, "The last one is DISCIPLINE—self-control. You discipline yourself. The difference between those who have an impact on lives and those who don't is simply that the latter group doesn't want it badly enough. Period. How badly do you want to be a man of God? Once you really understand God's grace and His unconditional love for you, the essence of living out Christianity is in the will."

The discipline Dr. Hendricks talked about is not about legalistic training in our own power and strength. It's about what we do with the righteousness we've been given. And the will is not just willpower. The mechanism of desire within us—our will—gets transformed. We have been given all we need, but we must choose by God's power to say yes to righteousness and no to the impulses of our flesh and the temptations all around us. As we continue to renew our minds with God's Word, our deepest longings are really being changed. We live out our faith because we want to, because we can, because we know who we are, because we have a vision of what God is calling us to be and do, and because He has provided everything necessary to make it possible.

Sometimes we aren't very honest with each other or ourselves. We say we want to be men and women of God, a loving husband or wife, a great parent, etc., but we really mean we want to be that kind of person as long as it doesn't interfere with our lives, our entertainment, our hobbies, or our relationships too much. A big part of putting off the old, renewing the mind, and putting on the new is making the definitive choice to live according to the vision God has given us.

I had gone to lunch thinking I was a man for God with a long "to do" list each day. I came back realizing I needed to be man of God with a focused "to be" list each day.

I left that conversation with Dr.

Hendricks and my peers with a challenge, and my life has never been the same. I stopped at a Dairy Queen on my way home that day and wrote my life objectives on a napkin: *I want to be a great man of God, I want to be a great husband, I want to be a great father, I want to be a great friend, I want to be a great pastor . . . in God's eyes.* I realized that if I really wanted to be a man of God, I would need to reorganize my life and heart. I wrote a brief plan and put those priorities in my weekly schedule. I had been a Christian with my own agenda—big plans and big dreams, but no clear target. Now I had one. I had gone to lunch thinking I was a man *for* God with a long "to do" list each day. I came back realizing I needed to be man *of* God with a focused "to be" list each day. I had been much too focused on myself and not nearly focused enough on God's grace.

Your Lifelong Renewal

Your encounters with God's truth will reorient your thoughts and perspectives, and they will always fit into the categories of putting off the old, renewing the mind, and putting on the new. You will come across things in yourself that need to be put in the "delete" folder, and the Holy Spirit will always engage you at points of renewal and restoration of God's image in you. What habits, temptations, thought patterns, and behaviors do you need to decisively break off and leave behind? In what ways do you need to see, think, and believe differently to conform to God's perspective? What do you need to add to your life that will make you more like Jesus? That's your lifelong process of transformation.

As with the caterpillar's transformation into a butterfly, you may not always be able to observe the change as it happens; the Holy Spirit works in the depths of our hearts, covered by the cocoon of our outward selves. But even when you don't, you will look back later and see it. The before-and-after pictures of your life will show a clear contrast. The new creation comes forth through our struggle of putting off the old self, allowing our minds to be renewed, and wearing our newness as if we were spreading our wings to take flight.

CHAPTER 8

How Do You Make It Last?

EPHESIANS 4:25-32

Throughout this book, you've read stories of people who have been frustrated with a lack of change in their lives. Many began struggling soon after they came to Christ and found help in the community of believers around them. Others have struggled, failed, inched forward, taken steps backward, and felt hopelessly stuck for years. But what if your experience has lasted decades? What if the process of change has felt so fruitless and seems so lost in the past that it's almost irrelevant now? Is there any hope for someone stuck in a long pattern of trying hard, doing good, and then failing?

Of course there is. But whether you have been struggling for a few months or many years, you need to know that some changes require more than new spiritual insights about our new identity and our best efforts. Some require a process that involves both time and intentional practice called "spiritual training."

We all have deeply embedded patterns in our thinking, attitudes, and behaviors that have been formed over many years. These patterns are highly resistant to change, and even when change begins to occur, we seem to default back into them under pressure.

I came across this principle of spiritual training at a time when my best and most intense efforts to break my workaholic, rushed, and overextended lifestyle were met with one failure after another. I had been a pastor of growing churches for more than ten years at the time, but after brief seasons of success I found myself exhausted, overextended, and living under constant stress and hurry. I happened to listen to a message by Dallas Willard in which he said spiritual transformation is impossible unless you "ruthlessly eliminate hurry from your life." He then talked about going into training to live an unhurried life. It was a foreign concept to me, but for two years, in desperation, I drove in the slow lane in traffic, got in the longest line at the grocery store, and decided to arrive at airports thirty minutes earlier than normal to eliminate the stress in getting there.

It wasn't easy to discipline myself to do those things with my type A personality and my deeply ingrained misbelief that "my value is determined by my productivity," but over a period of a couple years, my pace changed, my mental outlook changed, and my quality of life drastically improved. What I couldn't do, even though I was renewing my mind with God's Word, learning my new identity in Christ, and giving it my best effort, was accomplished by adding the aspect of spiritual training.

In many respects, spiritual training works a lot like physical training. For example, many people have the physical capacity within them to run the 26.2 miles of a marathon. But very few people would be able to do that tomorrow with any hope of finishing the race. No amount of trying hard, sweating, and wanting to finish, even for the highest purpose possible, would allow someone to accomplish what he or she hasn't prepared for. Some things require us to go into training to be successful. We already have everything we need within us, but our muscles require time, practice, and nutrition over a period of time in order to grow in strength to be able to run 26.2 miles. The capabilities we've been given need to be developed.

I saw this play out in real life several years ago. Amy, a woman in our church in her midforties, wanted to run a marathon. It was a genuine desire and, in theory, completely doable. But she had never been a runner. So Andrea, another church member who was an experienced runner in many marathons, offered to train her.

Amy knew she couldn't show up on the day of the race and try to run twenty-six miles. That wouldn't have worked, no matter how hard she tried. Her failure wouldn't mean she was a bad person or incapable of running. It would have meant only that she hadn't trained. To fulfill her desire, she would have to cooperate with the abilities of her body and her friend's coaching to turn potential into reality. So before they started, Andrea promised to develop a plan and hold Amy accountable to it. She reminded Amy that she already had everything she needed—strong lungs, strong legs, and a deep longing to accomplish her goal. And for five months, they trained together. They determined the right amount of sleep, adhered to a strict nutrition plan, eliminated distracting activities, and got to work.

The workouts began with a little walking and jogging, then mile-long runs, then longer runs of five, ten, and fifteen miles. It wasn't easy, and Amy had to give herself a lot of grace along the way. But her muscles strengthened, her lungs expanded, she developed the mental discipline to overcome pain, and she accomplished what had previously been impossible for her. She didn't start out trying hard to run a marathon. She built up to it, and on the day of the race, she went the entire distance. Andrea and Amy together had brought out the marathoner in Amy much like God brings out the image of Jesus in us.

I cannot express how important it is to understand this difference between trying hard to be holy and going into training. Yes, we must always give our very best effort as Scripture commands us, but it isn't just up to us, and it isn't instantaneous—or even quick. God has given us all that we need for life and godliness, but that doesn't mean it comes automatically or without a process. I learned this the hard way in a very challenging time with one of my sons.

Why Trying Hard to Be Holy Doesn't Work

When one of my sons was about fourteen, his struggle with a particular sin kept him in a constant cycle of failure, guilt, remorse, resolve to do better, and then failure again. He wanted to change, and he tried hard to do whatever it took to make it happen. I told him the importance of putting off the old, renewing our minds, and putting on the new. I helped him memorize Bible verses that might encourage and strengthen him. I explained the process of transformation we've been exploring in this book. But the results were always the same. That persistent sin would return, and my son would give in to it in moments of weakness and then lie about it, creating more conflict between us.

During one of our talks, he burst into tears. "I'm sorry, Dad. I'm sorry, I'm sorry. I'm trying as hard as I can. No matter how hard I try, I can't seem to overcome this. What else can I do?"

As his tears flowed and his frustration was turning into despair, God spoke to me in a flash of insight. I realized I had failed to teach him one of the most important lessons of spiritual transformation. I prayed about it for a day or two, then told my son I'd pick him up from school so we could spend time together. I told him to stop by the gym and put on workout clothes before he met me. But he had no idea where we were going.

We went to a fitness center owned by a good friend. We walked through the building and saw row after row of weight machines.

The place was crowded with bodybuilders of various ages displaying bulging muscles and popping veins. Some were lifting massive, bar-bending weights. My son was impressed.

We found an unoccupied bench press, and I introduced my son to the object lesson God had given me when we were talking about his struggles. He had seen his brothers lift weights, so he knew how it worked. But he hadn't done much of it himself. After a few warm-ups, I put a little more weight on his bar than I figured he could handle. He lowered the bar to his chest, then tried to lift it back up. About halfway, his arms started shaking. He kept trying, but it wouldn't go any higher.

I kept coaching him: "Try harder, son. Try harder!"

"I'm trying, Dad," he whimpered, as the bar began to wobble and sink back toward his chest. I intervened, lifted it up, and put it back on the stand. He was completely exhausted—and a bit confused.

"Did you try as hard as you could to lift that bar?" I asked.

"Yes, Dad. I promise, I tried as hard as I could."

"Then why couldn't you lift it?"

"Because I'm not strong enough," he said.

We sat in silence for a moment, surrounded by men who had spent hours upon hours developing their strength. Then I brought the point home. "Based on what we just did, are you willing to agree that there are certain things you can't do simply by trying?"

The lights came on in his eyes. He realized we were talking about more than weightlifting.

I pointed to a couple of heavy lifters nearby. "Do you think those guys could lift three hundred pounds the first time they tried?"

"No."

"Then how are they able to do that now?"

"I don't know."

"By going into training."

"If you came in here three times a week for three months, wouldn't you be able to lift more than you can lift today?"

"Yeah, Dad. I'm sure I could."

We talked about the futility and limitations of trying hard when you don't have enough strength. I assured him that he already had the means, but it needed to be developed. He would have to work up to what he wasn't able to do right now. I reminded him that life is full of challenges that no one can overcome by self-effort alone. But we can master them by going into training to appropriate the grace God has already given us.

We've looked at the basic principles of transformation—putting off, being renewed, and putting on. I've encouraged you to look at the places in your life that God is targeting for change and think about how to apply these principles. Much of what we've talked about is foundational, but if you're like me, you need some starting points for applying God's Word. In this chapter, we turn to the role of spiritual training, one of the most important lessons you can learn about the way God transforms lives. It's also one of the most neglected and misunderstood aspects of spiritual growth. If we don't grasp the role of spiritual training, we will likely continue to be frustrated or fall into despair like my son.

So far, we've learned that:

- Every believer is called to be transformed (Eph. 4:1–6).
- Christ's defeat of sin, death, and Satan makes transformation possible (Eph. 4:7–10).
- The church is God's primary agent of transformation in our lives (Eph. 4:11–16).
- We achieve personal purity by God's threefold principles of transformation: put off the old, be renewed, and put on the new (Eph. 4:17–24).

We have everything we need to live a Christlike life. Christ lives within us by His Holy Spirit and has given us His Word, His promises, and His people. But we must go into intentional spiritual training to grow our spiritual muscles so our beliefs and behavior continually align more as we grow to maturity.

God's Training Program

In Ephesians 4:25–32, Paul fleshes out the threefold principles of transformation into five areas of spiritual training. I believe the sequence of these five areas is intentional. They represent specific aspects of our lives in which God wants to produce continual transformation, core issues where spiritual training becomes a catalyst for real change.

> Therefore each of you must put off falsehood and speak truthfully to your neighbor, for we are all members of one body. "In your anger do not sin": Do not let the sun go down while you are still angry, and do not give the devil a foothold. Anyone who has been stealing must steal no longer, but must work, doing something useful with their own hands, that they may have something to share with those in need.
>
> Do not let any unwholesome talk come out of your mouths, but only what is helpful for building others up according to their needs, that it may benefit those who listen. And do not grieve the Holy Spirit of God, with whom you were sealed for the day of redemption. Get rid of all bitterness, rage and anger, brawling and slander, along with every form of malice. Be kind and compassionate to one another, forgiving each other, just as in Christ God forgave you. (Eph. 4:25–32)

It begins with personal integrity (v. 25). God desires truth in our innermost being. If we can't be honest with ourselves, with God, and with others, real transformation will never occur.

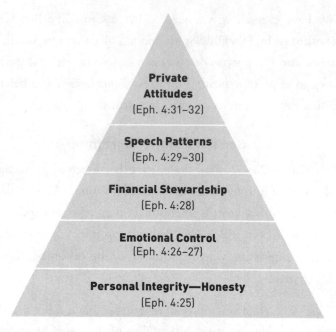

Paul compared godliness to athletic discipline on several occasions (1 Cor. 9:25–27; 1 Tim. 4:8; 2 Tim. 2:5). Though there are significant differences, there are also some similarities. Just as a good exercise program begins with the core, stretches and strengthens the muscles around it, and expands cardiovascular capacity, our spiritual training begins with core attributes, stretches and strengthens the new nature within us, and shapes our hearts. Sometimes we feel as if we are being pushed to the limits, but the goal is to reflect and restore our original design—to uncover the masterpiece our Sculptor already sees. We enter into training to transform into the people we are called to be.

The last part of Ephesians 4 is a clear spiritual training program, a plan that takes us to the exercise stations we've overviewed to address five significant areas of our lives. Our trainer is the Holy Spirit. Like a master artisan, He already sees the image we are becoming. As we move through this spiritual gym, remember the key difference between physical and spiritual transformation. In physical training, all the weight is in your hands, and progressively trying harder is imperative. In spiritual training, it isn't up to you to do all the work. You cooperate with your trainer, but He's the source of the change within you. You aren't trying harder; you are submitting to being trained.

Training Station 1: Personal Integrity

> *Therefore each of you must put off falsehood*
> *and speak truthfully to your neighbor,*
> *for we are all members of one body.*
>
> EPHESIANS 4:25

- **Training Objective:** Honesty (Personal Integrity)
- **Training Command:** "Speak the truth in love" (see Eph. 4:15, 25)
- **Training Actions:**
  Put off—falsehood
  Renew—recognition of shared membership in the body
  Put on—truthful speech
- **Training Apparatus:** Practice Confession

You may notice a familiar pattern that will be repeated throughout this section: put off, be made new, and put on. This verse echoes Paul's instructions in the last passage to put off the old (falsehood) and do something new (speak truthfully). The command focuses on our "neighbor"—fellow believers—because we are members of the same body. But it might as well apply to everyone we relate to. Dishonesty—which includes pretense, hypocrisy, and lying—is never appropriate for a Christian. As Paul wrote earlier, we speak the truth in love.

It isn't difficult just to speak the truth. Neither is it very difficult just to love people. But balancing truth and love is tricky. Overemphasis on truth may make us honest, but our honesty can damage the people we love. Overemphasis on love neglects the hard things that need to be said. What Jesus taught us about financial responsibility also applies to our stewardship of the truth: those who are faithful in small things will be faithful in much (Luke 16:10). In our training in honesty, it's good to start with the little things.

For example, notice your little exaggerations or half-truths that make you look better—blaming your lateness on traffic that wasn't really the problem, or rounding up figures to be more impressive. Early in my ministry, every time I rounded up figures in a sermon, my wife would ask me why I lied. I'd exaggerate the attendance at a service, and she'd call me on it. We laugh about those conversations now, but they represented a real tension. I was okay with loose facts, and she was uncompromising in her integrity. God wanted me to learn to be honest in the small things.

Many Christians have developed seemingly harmless patterns of dishonesty that become the roots of denial, rationalization, compromise, and self-delusion. Undergoing training in this area involves the elimination of "white" lies, exaggerations, and partial truths. One of the greatest helps for me has been practicing confession.

As I was learning the importance of truthfulness, I sometimes had to make awkward phone calls to people to correct or clarify some misstatements I'd made, and it wasn't easy. I once got a call from a representative from a major mission organization who was putting a basketball team together for ministry tours. I'd had a lot of experience at college basketball, and I still played in a league. I told this recruiter I was in my best shape ever, but when he asked how many points I was averaging, I started guessing, rounding up, and overestimating my stats. The league I was in didn't keep statistics, so I just started pulling them out of the air. I lied. And in my conversations with God about it afterward, I just couldn't get any peace. He wouldn't let it go. I eventually called this guy up, admitted making up my stats because I really wanted to be on the team, and asked his forgiveness.

When you know up front that you'll have to do that, you begin to tell the truth in everything, big or small. It's hard, but it's good for you. People begin to trust you more. You won't have to keep up any façades or illusions. You'll break the cycle of dishonesty and failure. Your integrity will flow from the inside out and earn the respect of others.

Training Station 2: Emotional Control

> *"In your anger do not sin": Do not let the sun go down while you are still angry, and do not give the devil a foothold.*
>
> EPHESIANS 4:26–27

- **Training Objective:** Emotional Control
- **Training Command:** "Be angry, and yet do not sin" (Eph. 4:26 NASB)
- **Training Actions:**
  Put off—anger that leads to offense and sin
  Renew—recognition of dangers in retaining anger
  Put on—appropriate expressions of anger
- **Training Apparatus:** "I Feel" Messages

Spiritual growth is often thwarted by emotional lives not controlled by the Spirit of God. "Human anger does not produce the righteousness that God desires" (James 1:20). Yet Paul clearly assumes we will be angry—some translations actually say to "be angry"—and that anger isn't necessarily sin. Since God expresses anger, we know it's not inherently evil. But what we do with our anger can be.

Again, we see the put off / put on dynamic. We put on righteous anger when necessary, but we put off whatever sin might follow it. Why? Because letting it linger gives the devil an opportunity. When someone cheats, steals, or otherwise treats you unfairly, go ahead and be angry. But don't give in to wounded pride or a bad temper. Bring it under control and express it in appropriate ways.

Anger gradually turns into a way of seeing the world and the people around you. That's one reason so many marriages deteriorate. Husbands and wives don't just wake up and decide to have an affair, walk away from the relationship, or avoid their commitments. They go to bed angry and, over time, start seeing each other through that anger. Unresolved anger can become a lasting condition of hurt feelings, withdrawal, and bitterness. And, as Paul said, this is one of the ways demonic activity enters into relationships.

Conversely, worship, gratitude, and grace turn into a much truer way of seeing. They create a climate for genuine forgiveness, which keeps resetting anger levels to zero and doesn't allow them to build up. Instead of hardened hearts, we live with soft hearts and open arms. The practice of confession works powerfully here too. When we own up to our part of a problem, no matter how minor that part was, forgiveness flourishes. "I was wrong," "I didn't listen," "I reacted defensively," "I could have done a better job of helping"— making statements like these before the sun goes down does wonders for our relationships.

If you're like me, you didn't learn how to resolve anger as a child. Not many of us did. But if you want your emotions to be under God's control, you'll need to know how. "I feel" messages are a wonderful tool for dealing with them appropriately. Early in our marriage, Theresa and I had trouble resolving our anger. We didn't yell or blow up at each other. I just got mad, and she withdrew.

After a day or two of her not talking and me being passive aggressive, we'd warm back up to each other, say we were sorry, and then start the cycle all over again next time.

Eventually, a counselor taught us not to send "you should" messages that provoke defensiveness in each other but to address our feelings. "I feel angry (or hurt, rejected, lonely) when you . . ." The other person can't argue with that; it's an honest feeling. And one day when I came home late—a chronic habit of mine—Theresa didn't get angry. She took the wonderful dinner she had prepared out of the refrigerator, warmed it up, waited for me to finish eating, and then told me very quietly and deliberately that she felt hurt and unloved when she spent that much time cooking a meal and I didn't show up or even call. She spoke the truth in love, and, now with my defenses down, I saw it through her eyes.

Most families have developed the habit of either attacking or not saying anything. Neither approach works. Stuffing and internalizing feelings eventually leads to a blowup. Lack of patience, emotional fallout, and other problems in relationships are training for life. Choose to become a person whose emotional lifestyle is under the Holy Spirit's control.

Training Station 3: Financial Stewardship

> *Anyone who has been stealing must steal no longer, but must work, doing something useful with their own hands, that they may have something to share with those in need.*
>
> EPHESIANS 4:28

- **Training Objective:** Financial Stewardship (Work Ethic)
- **Training Command:** "Steal no longer" (Eph. 4:28)

- **Training Actions:**

Put off—stealing

Renew—think differently about the value of work

Put on—work

- **Training Apparatus:** Good Mentors

Here Paul tells us to put off stealing and put on diligence. In the process, we renew our minds to think differently about work. What's the purpose? To be able to share with those in need.

Many of us grew up with a negative attitude toward work. You go in as late as possible, come home as early as possible, try do the minimum and get paid the maximum. Or if you own the company, you go in before dawn and come home after dark because work is all there is. Either way, it's about getting as much as you can out of your work life for your own sake. Along the way, find all the shortcuts you can.

That's not a biblical approach to work. Both the shortcut mentality and the work-yourself-to-death mentality are enemies to our transformation. One turns hopes toward get-rich-quick schemes and lottery miracles that almost always lead to disappointment. The other will crush your spirit.

Paul tells us to go into training in the area of diligence. He begins with a command to stop stealing—not a hypothetical situation in the Ephesian church—and to work hard with the needs of others in mind. If everyone is looking out for each other's needs, stealing is unnecessary. And if everyone is working diligently, no one suffers lack. But apart from having enough resources to live on, this concept points to a broader and deeper lifestyle. We can't live holy lives without doing our part. The shortcut mentality makes us want to skip the training, the deep conversations, the Bible studies and group accountability, the disciplined prayer times, and anything else that costs much time and effort. But anything that grows well and lasts will grow slowly. Oak trees take decades. Weeds come up overnight. Who do you really want to be?

Paul gives us a needed shift in our perspective in another passage. "Whatever you do, work at it with all your heart, as working for the Lord, not for human masters, since you know that you will receive an inheritance from the Lord as a reward. It is the Lord Christ you are serving" (Col. 3:23–24). Every moment of every day becomes an opportunity to turn the daily grind into personal worship. Whatever you do—filing papers, changing diapers, washing dishes, making sales calls, cutting the grass—becomes an occasion to display the love and character of God to people who really need to see Him. It's important not only because of the fruitfulness it can bring but because of the One who receives the offering. It makes every moment sacred.

Godly people do not experience transformation through shortcuts. They also don't receive it by taking all the responsibility upon themselves. They trust God and know their part in cooperating with Him.

Life easily becomes busy and overextended—kids in several sports or clubs per season, parents shuffling them all over the city, office hours that extend late into the evening, maintaining a lifestyle that puts us in the right neighborhoods, schools, and social circles. That's not diligence. Biblical diligence orders our priorities to serve God without suffocating ourselves. It's good, honest, hard work—not out just for more money and more stuff but for a deeper, purer, more fruitful relationship with God.

Godly diligence leads to genuine transformation and an amazing depth of life. Many of us need good models and mentors for this; observing the faithfulness and generosity of other Christians gives us a picture of how to turn work into worship and meet our own needs and the needs of others through what God provides.

But there is no substitute for it. See it not as drudgery but as an adventure. God rewards the faithfulness of those who serve Him diligently day after day.

Training Station 4: Positive Speech

> *Do not let any unwholesome talk come out*
> *of your mouths, but only what is helpful*
> *for building others up according to their needs,*
> *that it may benefit those who listen.*
> *And do not grieve the Holy Spirit of God, with*
> *whom you were sealed for the day of redemption.*
>
> EPHESIANS 4:29-30

- **Training Objective:** Positive Speech
- **Training Command:** "Say only what helps" (the message of Eph. 4:29)
- **Training Actions:**
  Put off—negative speech
  Renew—give grace to others and avoid grieving the Holy Spirit
  Put on—positive, encouraging speech
- **Training Apparatus:** Practice Silence and Solitude

The essence of Paul's message here is, "tame your tongue." Do not wound people with your words. Put off unwholesome speech and put on the words that build others up. Why? Because (1) positive, enriching words strengthen relationships and reflect God's nature; and (2) negative words grieve God's Spirit. God isn't an impersonal force. He has feelings. His heart can be broken. He doesn't want His precious children to be on the sharp end of wounding words. He wants us to use the gift of speech to pour out love, joy, encouragement, and blessing.

Words carry the power of life and death (Prov. 18:21). They can literally make or break someone's day. They can even ruin someone's life, especially if that person is young and looks up to us. Jesus was clear that what comes out of our mouths, whether good or evil, comes from whatever treasure is in our hearts (Luke 6:45). If you really want to take your spiritual temperature, don't look at your religious activities, your giving, or your morals. Listen to your words. According to Jesus, that's the clearest indication of where your heart is.

James wrote harshly about the way many Christians use their tongues and emphasized bringing our words under the Holy Spirit's control. If we can do that, we can bring our entire lives under the Spirit's reign (James 3:2). Jesus strongly warned against careless words too. We will have to give an account for them one day (Matt. 12:36). That's a sobering thought, and it makes me wish I could go back and undo all the sarcastic, flippant, cutting words I've ever spoken, especially to family members I love dearly. In our training, we will need to be extremely diligent about putting off words that wound and putting on words that bless and build up.

One of the best ways we can train ourselves in positive speech is to learn to practice silence and solitude. Sometimes we just need to talk less. Proverbs tells us that the more we talk, the more likely we are to sin and offend (10:19). That goes not only for our mouths but also our fingertips. We live in a toxic culture of complaint and criticism, and online conversations can turn vicious and degrading in a hurry. Don't get caught up in that kind of discussion, regardless of the forum.

I've been training a long time in this area, and sometimes I still have struggles. I've worked several practices into my life that have helped tremendously, and I think they could help you too. First, memorize James 1:19b–20: "Everyone should be quick to listen, slow to speak and slow to become angry, because human anger does not produce the righteousness that God desires." Having this truth in my heart helps me bite my tongue when I'm tempted to let it loose.

Also consider journaling three or four times a week in a quiet place. Sit silently before God and ask Him to highlight what's been coming out of your mouth the last two or three days. Then consider why—the motives, insecurities, fears, anxieties, and desires behind your words. Seeing these patterns in my motives has created opportunities for real growth. Finally, consider taking a personal retreat for a day or two every few weeks or months. I put aside work during these times and slow down. I walk, think, journal, pray, and rest. God reveals things that have come out of my mouth that I've long forgotten. I tell Him I'm sorry, and when appropriate, I go back and apologize to those I've offended. If I keep account of my words and take care of the consequences, I won't have to give an account to God for having an out-of-control mouth.

Training Station 5: Holy Private Attitudes

> *Get rid of all bitterness, rage and anger, brawling and slander, along with every form of malice. Be kind and compassionate to one another, forgiving each other, just as in Christ God forgave you.*
>
> EPHESIANS 4:31–32

- **Training Objective:** Holy Private Attitudes
- **Training Command:** "Be kind to one another, compassionate, forgiving each other, just as God in Christ also has forgiven you." (Eph. 4:32 NASB)
- **Training Actions:**
  Put off—hate

Renew—new attitudes based on what God has done

Put on—love

• **Training Apparatus:** The Matthew 5:24 Principle

Paul gives us a list of things to put off, and each one can be dealt with through a strong sense of grace and the practice of forgiveness. In fact, that's what he tells us to put on: kindness, compassion, and an awareness that the forgiveness we extend to others is a reflection of the forgiveness God has given us. More succinctly, we put off hate, renew our attitudes based on what God has done for us, and put on love.

Kindness and compassion cover a multitude of sins and offenses. The language suggests treating people as we would like to be treated ourselves and loving them with gut-level compassion. The result is forgiveness. While the world returns offense for offense and hurt for hurt, we break the cycle by treating people as Jesus would treat them. After all, we are being conformed to His likeness. Our impulse responses need to give way to His enduring love. We release people from whatever retaliation they might deserve, just as God has done with us.

That may not be easy when someone cuts you off in traffic, slights you socially or financially, or offends you with some callous remark. My tendency is to want justice to come down against everyone except me. Like most human beings, I have an eye-for-an-eye reflex that kicks in when I'm mistreated. But I want God to forgive me when I'm the offender rather than the offended, so I need to forgive as I want to be forgiven. God has already made a deal with us. His Son died on the cross for our sins, and our sinful behavior is already covered, paid for in full. As Jesus said, we need to freely give what we have freely received (Matt. 10:8). We can't choose to live in a culture of grace and mercy for ourselves and step out of it when others do something wrong. It's all or nothing. And when we believed, we entered into that culture.

Jesus' words in Matthew 5:23–24 are helpful for our training in this area: "If you are offering your gift at the altar and there remember that your brother or sister has something against you, leave your gift there in front of the altar. First go and be reconciled to them; then come and offer your gift." In other words, put your worship on hold until you seek reconciliation. Our normal approach is to wait for the other person to seek reconciliation, especially if we think that person is primarily responsible for the conflict. But God says the relationship is more important than figuring out who to blame. Take responsibility for your part, even if you think only 10 percent of it is on you, and go ask forgiveness for however you contributed to the conflict. That's much more important—and liberating— than holding out for someone else to confess and seek forgiveness.

Is that fair? Of course not. Neither was it fair when Jesus forgave you of all your sin. If He is living inside you, that same grace should be at work in your relationships. It isn't always easy to embrace that perspective, but no one said training for transformation would be easy. This is a big part of your journey in becoming like Him.

All of these training activities can be summed up in one instruction: let Jesus live His life in you. Little by little, the Holy Spirit on the inside will become visible on the outside. The figure of Jesus will begin to emerge from the rough block of stone that you submitted to the master Artist's hand. The sculpture is not completely finished until you see Him face-to-face—you will never be perfect this side of eternity—but you will experience significant, radical life-change. Transformation will become the norm in your life.

Made to Last

The power to change is in us from the first day of our relationship with Jesus to our last day on earth. It's available in full as soon as we believe in Him and begin our walk with Him, but learning to rely on that power and following God's training program can be a long process. In fact, God has done some of His greatest work in people who came to the party late—who thought they had missed their time of fruitfulness. No matter how many times you've started and stopped, no matter how long your frustrations have lasted, you are not too late. The miracle of life-change is still there for you to experience.

Great works of art often take an unusually long time. In the early 1460s, a sculptor named Agostino was commissioned to create a sculpture of David. It was to be part of a series of statues begun much earlier in the city of Florence under the direction of Donatello. A block of marble was cut from a quarry in the Alps, and Agostino began his work. But he didn't get very far. Donatello died in 1466, and the project seems to have been abandoned in the absence of his oversight. Another sculptor was hired about ten years later to continue the work, but he was terminated soon afterward, and the block of marble, now roughly shaped into the form of a human figure, sat unattended for twenty-six years.

Soon after the turn of the century, authorities contracted with a young artist named Michelangelo to complete work on this rough block of stone. For more than two years, Michelangelo formed this figure, diligently chiseling and grinding away everything that didn't look like David until a beautiful Renaissance image of the biblical hero emerged. The statue was placed in the public square in 1504—it took several days to move it just a half-mile from Michelangelo's workshop—and stood in the square for more than three centuries before being moved to a gallery. The masterpiece continues to capture the imagination and awe of many.

Have you ever thought of a sculpture from the perspective of the stone it is carved from? It doesn't create itself. It is chosen by the artist and submits to the artist's hands. If it could feel pain, it wouldn't always enjoy the process. But if it could see the end result in advance, it would endure for the glory to come. It would submit to the tools of the master. It couldn't turn the process into an instantaneous event, as if some explosion could break off the exterior in exactly the right places and reveal the form immediately. And it couldn't accomplish anything by trying harder. Ultimately, the results are up to the creator, not the stone.

Our transformation can be just as drawn out, unevenly paced, and meticulously finished as the process that turned an alpine stone into Michelangelo's classic statue. We come to our Master in the rough form of the image He originally gave us, but He works diligently to chip away and grind down every aspect of our being that doesn't conform to the image of Jesus. He does it with great care; no violent blows are accidental. And He also takes His time; the end result will be worth the patience and attention to detail. Unlike a block of stone, we do participate in the process. But we can't make it happen by trying harder; we have to let Him shape us. Eventually these rough blocks of stone are transformed, now visible as God's workmanship, monuments to His own image and testimonies of the restoration He offers to anyone who submits to His tools. In His hands, cooperating with His work by faith, we discover what we were made to look like.

Your transformation is more of an unveiling than a process of simply becoming. The real you has been there ever since you accepted Christ. Your new identity is written into your spiritual DNA, just as surely as Michelangelo's *David* was already hidden somewhere in that chunk of marble. The raw material of your life has to go through a long and sometimes uncomfortable process, but considering the craftsmånship of our Sculptor, it's in good hands. You do have to take off the old and put on the new, but the new is not foreign to you. It comes up from within you because that's where the Spirit of God dwells.

Your part in this journey is to appropriate His grace and power in the areas of personal integrity, emotional control, financial stewardship, positive speech, and private attitudes. Avoid focusing on failures; nowhere does Scripture tell us to focus on sin in order to overcome it. Your transformation depends on an entirely different focus—laying aside every weight, running the race, fixing your vision on Jesus, and letting that vision change you (2 Cor. 3:18; Heb. 12:1–2). Celebrate the victories, no matter how small. Always stir up hope. Remember what Paul told Timothy: "Be diligent in these matters; give yourself wholly to them, so that everyone may see your progress" (1 Tim. 4:15). God gives you plenty of grace, and you need to do the same. Don't take grace for granted, but apply it as often as needed. Embrace your training with joy.

That's where your transformation leads. Remember that, unlike natural bodybuilding, this is not just about you training yourself. God is the master craftsman. You are cooperating with Him by submitting to His tools and counsel. He has a lot at stake in your training; it began with the sacrifice of His Son and is made possible by the gifts He has given you and the believers who surround you with support. But He is committed to this process and will carry it on to completion (Phil. 1:6). He is the master craftsman at work on your soul, your number one training partner, coach, and cheerleader. You can trust Him every step of the way.

Conclusion

The story of change doesn't end with the last verse in Ephesians 4. Paul goes on to urge his readers to follow God's example, walk in the way of love, and live sacrificially as Jesus did (5:1–2). He follows that instruction with more practical examples of what the changed life looks like in terms of purity, speech, and relationships. He says to live as children of light and stay out of the darkness, being wise and filled with the Spirit. The implications of the changed life are far-reaching. But they all flow out of the foundation already laid in this letter.

I don't know where you are in your journey of transformation or how the truths in this book have affected you. But I do know that if you have read to the end, you are motivated and on the right track, and you have what you need to continue. The kingdom of God opens up before you as you live in your new identity, enter into the wonders of its culture and values, die to old ways in order to live in the new, engage in fellowship with other believers both to give and receive the spiritual gifts God has poured out, and allow yourself to be transformed, always walking that balance between training yourself for change and resting in the power that works within you. If you have placed your faith in Jesus, all things have become new. He has given you His own life. All that's left is to walk in it.

As we've seen, that's easier said than done. But it is nevertheless doable. You have the promises of God, the victory of Jesus, and the power of His Spirit. You can return to His Word again and again, allowing its truths to sink into your heart. You have the testimonies, experiences, and counsel of other Christians to learn from, lean on, and contribute to. And you have a calling that is backed by all of the above and, in your most honest moments, embraced by the longings of your own heart. You've got this.

And remember that He has you. As we've discussed, give yourself grace in the process. Don't abuse grace by using it as an excuse, but don't neglect it either. Every single person throughout history who has begun as a sinner, been redeemed, and grown into spiritual maturity has stumbled, fallen, gotten stuck, and needed help at times. Many of their stories are written in the pages of Scripture. You have plenty of company in the great cloud of witnesses of salvation history.

Remember too that God does not define you by your past or your present. He sees the new you, the vision of who you are becoming, the completed, purified soul that will live with Him forever. He knows the change that awaits you, and He sees the glory to come. Your job is to see that vision too—or trust it when you can't see it— and walk in that direction. You aren't trying to get adopted by God; you already have been (Eph. 1:5). You don't have to become a child of light; you already are one (Eph. 5:8). You aren't striving for spiritual blessings; they are already yours (Eph. 1:3). You have already been chosen to be holy and blameless (Eph. 1:4), and God is simply calling you forward, very patiently, into that destiny. You have the victory of Jesus and all the resources of the kingdom to back you.

Live with that awareness, know your privileged place in the story of God's great, cosmic purposes, enjoy the opportunity to reflect His glory, partner with His people and His Spirit in a united expression of His will, and give yourself the tools and the room to grow. You are a new creation. Spread your new wings and soar.

Acknowledgments

I would like to thank Joe Stowell, former president of Moody Bible Institute, and Greg Thornton, then head of Moody Publishers, for taking a chance almost two decades ago on a young pastor from California with only one previous title to his credit.

The biblical content of this book was first taught to an eager group of believers in Santa Cruz, California. As we studied Ephesians 4 together, their stories of radically changed lives by the power of the Holy Spirit became the inspiration of what you now hold in your hands. The book was subsequently translated in many languages and circled around the world, helping believers understand that "trying hard to be a good Christian" is no substitute for understanding our new position in Christ and the process whereby we access the supernatural power of the Holy Spirit for life change.

Now, thanks to Randall Payleitner, the Moody team, and the editing, innovation, and creativity of Chris Tiegreen, this foundational teaching for life change has been updated and improved. The core life-changing truth has not been altered but has been repackaged for today's audience in a way that makes it more accessible and practical to the challenges that believers old and young face today.

It's a rare privilege to get to take what I've learned about how "life change really happens" since first writing this book almost 20 years ago. I've included new insights from fellow pastors, teachers, books, experiences around the world, and the wisdom that comes with the personal hurts, sufferings, failures, false expectations, and pride that I've dealt with in my own life.

I'm particularly grateful for the encouragement and love from the vital communities that have practiced the principles in this book, especially in their application to me and my family. Words cannot express my deep appreciation for the people of Santa Cruz Bible Church, the Bridge Church, Walk Thru the Bible, Venture Christian Church, and of course, the amazing staff and transformational culture of my brothers and sisters at Living on the Edge.

Closer to home, I have lived with a woman of incredible devotion to the Lord and integrity with people. My wife, Theresa, walks with God in a way that has inspired and challenged me to practice what I preach and to live out of my new identity in Christ for over 40 years. My adult children Jason, Eric, Ryan, and Annie, along with their mates and little ones, have provided untold joy, more than a few needed rebukes, and a journey of "life change" that continues to this day.

So, in many ways, this book has been "reborn" by the lives and experiences of many brothers and sisters in Christ, all of whom are committed to God's grand purpose of "being conformed to His image" in order that we might love Him more deeply and others more authentically.

Notes

1. C. S. Lewis, "First and Second Things," in *God in the Dock*, ed. Walter Hooper (Grand Rapids, MI: William B. Eerdmans Publishing Co., 1970), 310.

2. There is no evidence that Gandhi actually ever said this, but something very similar was said by an early twentieth-century Indian philosopher. Regardless of the source, it very effectively captures the mindset of many people who have rejected Christianity based on the lives of Christians.

3. James 4:8 is a possible exception, where James urges the double-minded and proud to repent. In 1 Timothy 1:15, Paul seems to be referring to his background as a persecutor (cf. 1 Cor. 15:9). The New Testament almost always uses "sinner" to refer to our past or those who are not yet redeemed.

4. Rick Warren, *The Purpose Driven Life: What on Earth Am I Here For?* (Grand Rapids, MI: Zondervan, 2012), 149.

5. *The Daily Walk Bible* (Carol Stream, IL: Tyndale House Publishers, 2013).

6. Paul E. Little, *Know Why You Believe* (Downers Grove, IL: InterVarsity Press, 1968).

7. Paul E. Little, *Know What You Believe* (Downers Grove, IL: InterVarsity Press, 2003).

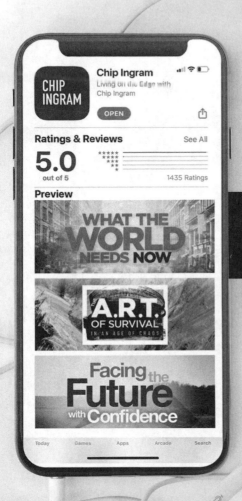

BIBLE STUDIES by
CHIP INGRAM

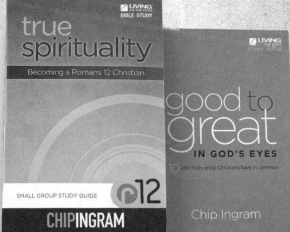

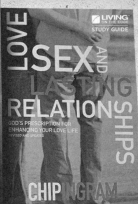

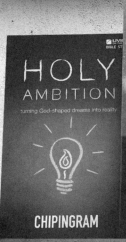

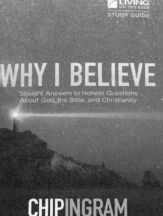

Available at LivingOnTheEdge.org

If the idea of walking with Jesus doesn't make you uncomfortable, you haven't thought seriously enough about His presence in your life.

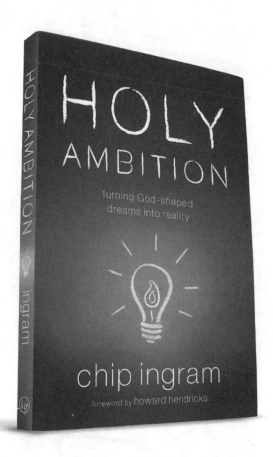